Trojan Goat
A self-sufficient house

W0116052

Winner of the Design and Livability Contest in the
U.S. Department of Energy's First Solar Decathlon

solarhome.lib.virginia.edu
www.solardecathlon.org

by John D. Quale
Assistant Professor
University of Virginia School of Architecture
Department of Architecture and Landscape Architecture

preface by Kenneth Frampton

05 04 03 02 01 54321 First Edition
ISBN 0-9771024-0-8
ISSN 1556-5483

Book design: Keith Godard, StudioWorks
Design assistant: Kamomi Solidum
Printed by Carter Printing, Richmond, VA
Distributed by University of Virginia Press

University of Virginia School of Architecture
Campbell Hall, P.O. Box 400122
Charlottesville, VA 22904
www.arch.virginia.edu

Table of Contents

In the team section of this book, I have attempted to recognize all the participants of this complex two-year long project. I've limited myself here to thanking those that contributed in some way to the production of this book.

Thanks to:

All the 'goats'—students from architecture, engineering, landscape architecture and planning—who made the house their own, and expanded the vision. I've learned a great deal from them.

Judith Kinnard, former department chair of architecture, for bringing me back to the School of Architecture, and for believing in my ability to take on the Solar Decathlon. A generous mentor, Judy provided guidance in the early thinking about the book.

Engineering Professor Paxton Marshall, for his calm demeanor, rigorous thinking and willingness to work with a bunch of architects.

Architecture Dean Karen Van Lengen, for supporting the project and allowing the Goat to be the first volume in the school's new series of books, *Urgent Matters*. Karen's vision for the book has helped me clarify the structure.

William Sherman, current chair of the Architecture and Landscape Architecture, for many things, but especially for his thoughtful mentoring and support.

School of Architecture Foundation Director Susan Ketron and Associate Dean Elizabeth Fortune for all sorts of help, including money.

Dan Pearce, for challenging everything.

Derry Wade, for her laser eye on the text.

My wife, Sara Osborne, for her patience, and Walker and Alice for letting a 'house called goat' be a part of our lives.

John D. Quale
Summer 2005

Acknowledgements

5

Introduction

Message from the Dean of the School of Architecture

In the life of a school and community there are touchstone events that recognize the core values of an institution and that exemplify their attributes and their ambitions. The 2002 Solar Decathlon had that quality for the School of Architecture at the University of Virginia. This book documents this winning project, its process and its product.

In the Fall of 2002, the U.S. Department of Energy sponsored a competition among academic institutions to design, build and display a modest 800 square foot house using innovative design and solar technologies in order to create the most energy efficient home for the future. The judging and the display of the 14 finalists' houses occurred one year after 9/11, a time when many Americans recognized the need to become more self sufficient and visionary in their design of sustainable environments for the future. This was indeed an historic moment and one in which the University of Virginia was proud to participate. As the competition unfolded on the Mall in front of the Capital, there was a palpable excitement and energy about the government's commitment to introduce the merits of solar energy to the nations people by placing these houses at its symbolic core. For two weeks after the judging, Americans were invited to tour the houses so that they might experience and potentially use these innovative ideas in their own communities.

Our University of Virginia team won first prize in design and second prize in overall energy efficiency. The prizes were shared by an interdisciplinary student and faculty team of architects, landscape architects, engineers and planners who worked together over a period of almost two years to create an aesthetic and technically sophisticated house. Our team's design approach acknowledged that the house of the future might not only perform differently but ought also to look and feel different than the standard developer home. The innovative use of light, the aesthetic reuse of historic materials and the house's potential to engage with its landscape and external conditions won it special recognition by Glenn Murcutt and other jurors.

As dean, I was extremely proud of the team, its process and its result. However I am even more pleased by the way this project has served to influence the trajectory of the school. For many years the School of Architecture has incorporated sustainable principles into its architecture, landscape architecture and planning curricula. Recently, we successfully defined new ways of collaborating and sharing our resources as in our newly integrated Department of Architecture and Landscape Architecture. We designed a sophisticated building technologies sequence in collaboration with our aesthetically renowned design studios. And as a result of our success in the Solar Decathlon, we have procured funding to support subsequent innovative housing design projects using sustainable principles. In addition, we have tapped our faculty expertise to design our own environment. Here at the School of Architecture, from outdoor classrooms and interior projects to the design of two new building additions and the redesign of our landscape, we are applying innovative design solutions using sustainable technologies and planning strategies. The solar house project represents a very important beginning that has given us national recognition for our efforts in the realm of design/build and sustainable design. I am pleased to introduce this project to you.

Karen Van Lengen
Dean and Edward E. Elson Professor

Preface

The Trojan Goat: A Distant Appraisal
by Kenneth Frampton

In an age such as ours the cause of sustainability is largely a guerilla operation; a sequence of endless skirmishes acted out in the face of the maximizing consumerist ideology of the powers that be. Of recent date nowhere has this been more ironically acknowledged than on the occasion of the Solar Decathlon staged in Washington, D.C. in the fall of 2002. In part to make a remarkable achievement better known and in part surely to make its critical/ethical position more readily accepted as a formative design discipline inside schools of architecture, this present publication documents the seminal contribution that was made to the Decathlon by a study team inside the School of Architecture and the School of Engineering at the University of Virginia, under the direction of John Quale and Paxton Marshall.

Appropriately tagged as the Trojan Goat, this house, designed and realized by both faculty and students, was exhibited on the National Mall along with a plethora of equally eco-sensitive model dwellings produced in a similar manner by thirteen other architectural schools across the country. It is naturally gratifying for the school that, in the subsequent expert evaluation of these full-size mock-ups, the UVA prototype should not only be rated first in terms of design and livability but also come in second with regard to all the other criteria including the engineering categories.

According to received statistics, buildings account for half the total energy burnt each year in the U.S., greater than that consumed per annum by automobile commutation. This remarkable fact plus the amount of land-fill produced by building waste makes it all the more relevant that the Trojan Goat should also have been constructed to a large degree out of recycled building material as well as being self-sufficient with regard to its use of passive energy.

To an outsider the palette of recycled materials ingeniously employed throughout this work borders on the exotic, above all surely the bluestone reclaimed from the paving around the Jefferson Rotunda on the UVA campus, and the salvaged copper roofing, the standing seams of which have to be flattened before being re-bent to form the horizontal lap joints necessary to sheath the house in copper. There is something knowingly Semperian about protecting this extravagant metal surface with a "woven," rain shield made up of red oak slats, salvaged from discarded shipping palettes. The adjustable louvers poised in front of the long glass wall to the living room were painstakingly fashioned out of the same salvaged material; that is to say out of packaging material normally thrown out wholesale every day. And yet within the range of the recycled material incorporated into the house there is nothing that quite equals for luxurious effect the recycled glass tile used for the walls of the bathroom.

A serious disadvantage of all this from the point of view of demonstrating a sustainable house that could serve as a prototype for future ecological ex-urban development is that all these recycling procedures are extremely labor intensive, particularly when it comes to flattening copper or machining packing timber in order to convert such raw material into well-finished components. It is a sobering fact that while they are studying, architectural students represent an extremely cheap, intelligent and replenishable pool of labor; a "learning through doing" workforce which is not readily available in the outside world.

More replicable perhaps is the fact that in the Trojan Goat the whole concept of sustainability was extended beyond the one-off recycling of waste building material, to include the collection of storm water from the roof for the dual "grey water" purpose of irrigating plants and flushing toilets. This bio-organic approach is built into the design of the partially "green" roof, where a patent, hydro-tech waterproof membrane simultaneously facilitates both focused irrigation and the drainage of plants. In fact, most if not all Peter Buchanan's ten green precepts as set forth in his *Ten Shades of Green* exhibition catalogue (2000/2005), held under the auspices of The Architectural League of New York, are deftly adhered to in this diminutive 750-square-foot building, including use of precisely engineered timber from sustainably managed forests, which is employed here for the structural framework and the sub-flooring. A similar ecological concern is evident in the minimal use of toxic substances and the deployment wherever possible of processes that minimize waste, as in the rolled plywood birch veneer used for the lining of the ceilings and the walls. In general the house frequently makes an opportune use of materials which incrementally heighten its performance throughout, from the use of new forms of insulation such as sprayed-on foam, along with the complimentary use, where needed, of translucent double layered curtains. Lastly there is the deployment of flat bamboo for the floor which, apart from its svelte finish, is as durable as oak.

When it comes to the livability factor, the rubric under which the Trojan Goat surpassed all the other houses, everything stems from the elegant and ingenious planning of an open, single-story one bedroom dwelling. This is surely a microcosmic demonstration of what could also be achieved, with even greater benefit, in a larger family unit. Nowhere is this potential more rhetorically evident than in the so-called "sunspace" which, when opened, sits partially within and partially without the main body of the house. In winter or in inclement weather the half that lies under the roof may be appropriated, as it were, by closing two steel framed plate-glass doors set to either side of the sun terrace, thereby bringing the master bedroom within the total fluid volume of the house.

The one feature that ultimately conditions both the rhythmic order and ergonomic workability of this house is surely the "thick" north wall, which embodies in one continuous spatial layer the bathroom, the main bedroom closet, the entry hall, the kitchen, the refrigerator and general storage, plus a small study corner at the very end of the narrow spatial sequence. Interspersed within this layer, as a series of recesses accessible from the exterior, is the essential technological equipment, including all the various service runs for the plumbing and drainage and for the photovoltaic heating, cooling and lighting, plus two full-height cylindrical cisterns for the storage of rainwater. This thick wall is paralleled by the main passageway through the house, which, aside from providing for a band of zenithal, natural and artificial lighting in the ceiling, also determines the width of the windows at the two opposing ends of the corridor.

Surprisingly enough, given the exemplary achievement, this is a somewhat inadequately detailed document, for this work is a technological *tour de force* which possesses a potential that goes well beyond the confines of a small house. Does one detect in this otherwise inexplicable lapsus a decidedly unfashionable technological modesty or is it a question of guarding one's trade secrets?

Whatever the explanation may be, this house incorporates an exceptionally wide range of highly sophisticated techniques, including, however eccentrically, an adjustable photo-voltaic monopitch roof capable of being lowered into the horizontal position so as to reduce the overall height of the house when mounted on a flat bed truck, in order to clear the overpasses on the route from Charlottesville to Washington, D.C.

Apart from the passive solar heating and cooling and a heat pump chiller capable of dehumidifying the house through cooling registers in the ceiling, the two most visible eco-tech elements are the luminaire reflector dish on the roof and an LED so-called "smart wall" in the entry to the house. This spectacular device, glowing red when the house is too warm and blue when it is too cool, is capable of affording the occupant touch-screen control over the environmental systems in such a way as to enable one to maintain a constant balance between the inside and outside environments. This is a level of feedback that not even Glenn Murcutt has attempted in his expensive, "yacht-like," sustainable houses. Equally inventive and sophisticated from a technological standpoint is the idea of conducting natural light down from the roof into the house via an optical glass fiber cable that amplified by an etched glass tube might be able, according to the romance of the text, to simulate the effects of natural light after sunset. Surely one borders here on an exoticism which causes one to question the wider critical implications of the exercise. One recalls Tomas Maldonado's injunction against "an ideology of waste" that arises only too spontaneously in our technologically mesmerized society.

Notwithstanding such reservations one can only have praise for such an exceptional enterprise and for the didactic theme of sustainable habitation as a unifying pedagogical theme behind UVA's hands-on training. Under the leadership of the dean, Karen Van Lengen, and chairs Judith Kinnard and William Sherman, sustainable thinking has been carefully integrated into the UVA design curricula of both architecture and landscape architecture. Lastly there is the pointed use of warm, reassuring materials throughout, which accords to the work a level of psycho-social acceptability that is only too rare in prototypical designs by progressive architects.

Where in terms of critical environmental practice we should go from here is another matter entirely, given the obdurate hostility of the American home building industry to any kind of seriously sustainable development, accompanied by the equally stubborn refusal on the part of the petro-chemical industry along with rampant land speculation to brook any legal constraint over their insatiable appetite for consuming oil and simultaneously perpetuating the devastating kitsch of urban sprawl ad infinitum. For this is a dark time not only for the maintenance of a homeostatic environment but also for the survival of the species as a whole. The blanket rejection of the Kyoto Protocol is symptomatic of the corporate power under which we live; the mindless mark of an hegemonic elite which seemingly has little regard for either democracy or truth, in a land where 1% of the population owns 42% of its wealth and where at a global scale we continue to use (or should we say abuse?) 25% of the world's non-renewable resources while spewing out 21% of its pollution.

Prologue

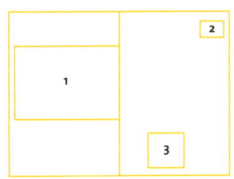

1
Visitors to the UVA house on the first day open to the public

2
Energy Secretary Spencer Abraham at the ribbon cutting ceremony

3
Washington, DC area school children check out the interactive displays at the Solar Decathlon event

Architecture

The designed environment is made of things we can see, hear, smell, touch and even taste. Collectively, our perceptions of these phenomena shape and define our aesthetic experience of architecture. Yet buildings and landscapes are dynamic systems that deeply influence society and ecosystems. While it is clear to some that architecture operates in the scientific, ecological, financial and social realms, a portion of contemporary architectural theory is focused purely on aesthetics: methods of form-making and composition. Architecture is deeply embedded in aesthetic issues, but discussions of architecture focused exclusively on form only serve to limit the potential of the discipline. Buildings should succeed not only aesthetically, but also technically, environmentally, socially and economically. Deliberate consideration of all these issues must be integral to the design process.

We begin the 21st century with the recognition that the building construction and operation sector of the U.S. economy depletes more fossil fuels than any other.[1] Not surprisingly, the U.S. is also generating the most greenhouse gas emissions.[2] The average single-family home in the U.S. emits more than 22,000 pounds of carbon dioxide

each year (from the electricity generated by utilities to run the home, and oil or gas powered appliances and equipment in the home).[3] This is more than twice the amount emitted by the typical American car. The reality is that inefficient McMansions are more harmful to the environment than gas guzzling SUVs.

The sun is the source of almost all forms of energy on the earth—from fossil fuels such as natural gas and petroleum, which become depleted over time, to renewable forms of energy such as biomass, wind, and solar power. In fact, each day the sun directly radiates more than 10,000 times the amount of energy required in the world.[4] Efficient and environmentally benign methods of harvesting solar radiation are clearly the wave of the future.

As it becomes increasingly clear that architects and engineers must take greater responsibility for the environmental consequences of their creative effort, studies are beginning to demonstrate that building design can impact everything from the quality of public health to the ability of students to succeed in the classroom.[5] There is a growing realization that buildings, nature and humans are inextricably connected.

I always urge my students to recognize this interdependence. I ask them to be simultaneously intuitive and rigorous, poetic and practical—to act as an artist and a scientist. I believe there is fertile ground in the blended field of architecture, where one can find intellectual rigor in formal composition and creative inspiration in scientific principles. I challenge my students to think of design issues from a variety of viewpoints—and encourage them to articulate aesthetic, technical, ecological, social and financial justifications for their ideas.

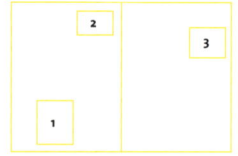

A Land Ethic

As a Wisconsinite, I was drawn during my undergraduate days to the writing of Aldo Leopold, a conservationist, scientist and author of "A Sand County Almanac." His concept of a land ethic has deeply influenced many environmentalists since it was first published in 1949. Embedded in his subtle and thoughtful observations on the flora and fauna of an ecosystem in central Wisconsin, Leopold establishes a framework for resolving the conflict between the demands of the economic marketplace and the simultaneously fragile and robust systems of nature.

"All ethics so far evolved rest upon a single promise: that the individual is a member of a community of interdependent parts. His instincts prompt him to compete for his place in the community, but his ethics prompt him also to co-operate...the land ethic simply enlarges the boundaries of the community to include soils, waters, plants and animals, or collectively: the land."[6]

Aldo Leopold

While much of his essay still resonates in the 21st century, I have concerns about the degree to which Leopold depends on society's eventual adoption of his land ethic to make any real progress on environmental

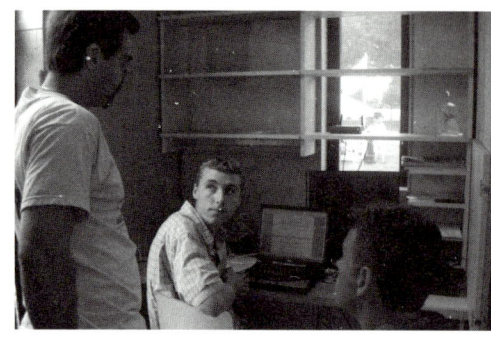

issues. For Leopold, it was "inconceivable" that a land ethic could thrive in modern society where we are increasingly separated from nature. One can only imagine what he would think if he were alive today—with the rapid suburbanization of the countryside, and the incredible technological advances since the mid-20th century. He goes so far as to say that "economic feasibility limits the tether of what can and cannot be done for land. It always has and always will."[7] He argues that as a society we must find value in the "uneconomic aspects" of land use, and makes a case for a "biotic" community whose health is determined by things that preserve its "integrity, stability and beauty."[8] In a sense, he says that if the economics argument fails, we have to encourage society to value ethics more.

Perhaps I am more of a pragmatist. I cannot see why the "tether" of economic feasibility has to be such a significant problem (although it certainly is in today's society). I would instead argue for a more thorough and thoughtful cost benefit analysis that rigorously addresses ecological, technical, aesthetic and social issues—along with the financial ones. Rather than finding value in the "uneconomic aspects" of nature, we need to more clearly demonstrate nature's true economic value. We cannot depend on society to come around to Leopold's land ethic by choice. American society tends toward simplistic answers where more sophisticated ones are often required. But if we can make the economic consequences of environmental devastation visible and undeniable to our contemporary society, we might have a chance for real change.

Designers and researchers are developing tools to make this happen. The evolving fields of life cycle analysis and ecological footprinting are the beginnings of an attempt to bridge economics and ecology. This area of research is still emerging, and the metrics are often imprecise. One problem is that it's difficult to operate in this realm without making direct comparisons between specific options—forcing designers to determine what is "less bad." Comparisons are difficult to make across scales of operation, or between radically different materials. When assembled as a structure, building materials are not simply inert, but components in dynamic systems. For example, the manufacturing process for many highly efficient insulation materials requires an intensive use of energy and dangerous chemicals. Yet when they are used properly, the benefits of increased energy efficiency can outweigh the negative environmental aspects. Bamboo flooring is a rapidly renewable material, the use of which could reduce demands on slow growing forests. Much of it, however, is shipped to the U.S. from half way around the world in China, and is assembled with urea formaldehyde binding agents, which negatively impact indoor air quality. Is it better than wood from a regional source that has been certified 'sustainable'? The answers require complex critical thinking, and ultimately, all building harms the environment in some way.

Architect William McDonough and scientist Michael Braungart imagine a world where all building materials have multiple lives, without any negative environmental impact. In contrast to the conventional practice of material resources flowing from original use to disposal—cradle to grave—McDonough and Braungart imagine a never-ending cycle of material "nutrient flows." They propose a "cradle to cradle" strategy where "products can be composed either of materials that biodegrade and become food for biological cycles, or of technical materials that stay in closed-loop technical cycles, in which they continually circulate as valuable nutrients for industry."[9]

While I have enormous respect for the ideas of McDonough and Braungart (and even briefly worked for McDonough's office when

it was in New York City), the world they imagine does not yet exist. We should do everything we can to achieve this extraordinary vision of the future, but we also have to recognize that buildings today are built mostly of materials without these amazing powers. Both idealism and pragmatism must guide our design processes.

Many designers today believe in the importance of "sustainable design." They might specify a few green building materials or select an energy efficient mechanical system. More than a few have vague intentions, but very little understanding of how to have a positive impact. Intuition about the importance of these issues must be matched by a rigorous understanding of how to make a difference. Legitimate methods for assessing the environmental impact of a given architectural design are still evolving, but that shouldn't stop practitioners and design students from striving.

Solar Decathlon

Students are searching for opportunities to turn their evolving ideas about sustainability into reality, and test them in the real world. The U.S. Department of Energy (DOE) started a design competition in 2000 to encourage students to do exactly that.

A team of architecture and engineering students at the University of Virginia recently participated in the first-ever Solar Decathlon. A national competition to design and build an 800 square foot house powered entirely by the sun, the Solar Decathlon brought together fourteen universities from across the U.S. to compete in ten events focused on energy-efficient house design. The teams assembled their houses on the

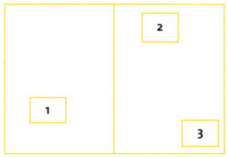

National Mall in Washington DC for three weeks in the fall of 2002.

Over the course of two years, more than 100 students spent countless hours designing, debating and building. They collaborated on all aspects of the process—from schematic design to construction, from fundraising to equipment specification. The School of Architecture and the School of Engineering and Applied Science integrated the project into their curricula, so that students could work together in and out of the classroom to put theories of sustainability into practice. Along the way, they were forced to question their ideas about "sustainable" design.

Architects and Engineers

Architects and engineers are in a unique position to operate in the interdependent world of buildings, society and nature. Trained to imagine their problems at multiple scales, and find the connections between those scales, both disciplines are constantly challenged to synthesize complex information and propose solutions. Engineers, grounded in the rigor of scientific

inquiry, and architects, driven by an iterative creative process, have the ability to study a problem from multiple perspectives.

Despite the similarities, architectural and engineering education is quite distinct. Engineers are taught principles and asked to solve problems with specific and knowable answers. Engineering students can display extraordinary creativity in the methodology for solving the problem, but the answer is still considered to be objectively 'right' or 'wrong.' Architectural education is about exploration—both of questions and of

answers. Operating within an inherently subjective discipline, architecture students are challenged to reframe assignments for themselves—often ignoring the initial assumptions. Conceptual clarity and critical thinking are as important as visual skills in architectural design. There are not any right or wrong design solutions.

Government Guidelines

These differences between the disciplines played out for the UVA team in the context of the competition guidelines, mostly written by government engineers. Although they were extremely professional individuals, with good intentions, the competition organizers had little interest in or knowledge of the architectural design process. They were constantly refining their criteria in an effort to make them more 'objective' (even when the result could actually increase the environmental impact of the competition, rather than decrease it). They sincerely believed there was a way to objectively judge architectural design—preferably with a checklist (just imagine: #37, conceptual and formal linkage between building form and small scale detail, √). On some level, several of the organizers were less than enthusiastic about creativity in architectural design, and probably expected the final designs to resemble standard single wide trailers. Of the fourteen schools, several did not have representation from architecture students. For the teams formed exclusively from engineering students, the results met the organizers' expectations.

I questioned organizers whether it was possible to hold a university house design competition without the required participation of architecture students. Wouldn't all teams benefit from collaboration between the disciplines? In addition it seemed to me that all teams should be required to address the issues inherent in the disciplines of landscape architecture and planning. How sustainable is a society where we all live in disconnected suburbs— living off renewable energy, but digging up green fields to replace them with roads, cars and solar houses? Isn't the issue of density versus sprawl worth discussing in a national competition?[10]

And what about affordability? We spent over $300,000 to design, build and transport our 750-square-foot house. That's $400 per square foot. Obviously, construction costs are rising across the country, but how does anyone justify that kind of spending for anything other than a prototypical design in a university competition intended to demonstrate expensive technology, and perhaps expand our collective thinking?

We were not able to convince the DOE officials to consider affordability in the final guidelines. Ultimately, we made a conscious choice to take on the competition guidelines quite literally. We hoped to prove we could play their game on our terms, and we were able to raise enough money to do so.

Perhaps most surprising was the fact that the event organizers seemed mostly focused on demonstrating renewable energy— in the very specific form of photo-voltaics. There were no points for other forms of renewable energy, natural ventilation, collection or storage of heat gain, or daylighting of interior spaces, let alone use of materials with reduced environmental impact. The houses built by UVA, University of Texas at Austin, Carnegie Mellon University, Virginia Polytechnic and State University, Auburn University and the University of Puerto Rico were the only ones to take a rigorously broader interpretation of environmental responsibility than the one offered by the DOE. It could also be noted that each of those schools included architecture students in their teams.

All of the teams recognized that it is difficult to define what is truly sustainable. I think it is accurate to say that we only had provisional strategies for making decisions on environmental issues. The DOE guidelines were certainly not definitive, but neither were those of any university team.

I took it upon myself to insist that architectural ideas be more integral to the competition than they were in the first draft of the rules. Although I had hoped to have an equal balance of points for architectural and engineering issues (the first draft had 100 points for 'design and livability' of the original 1000), I succeeded in getting the organizers to double the architecture points (making it 200 out of 1100 points in the final rules). I pushed for respected designers to be included in the architecture jury. Ultimately, the organizers selected judges with sophistication on environmental issues in architecture, two of whom also have national or international reputations as designers— Steve Badanes and Glenn Murcutt. With endless emails and long multi-team conference calls, the architecture advisors at the other universities and I were able to make incremental progress.

On some level it felt like the DOE considered architects to be the window dressers for the solid engineering strategies they wanted to demonstrate. It was clear that poetry and pragmatism could not easily co-exist in the halls of a sprawling government agency.

Despite my misgivings and frustrations, I have to say that the DOE and National Renewable Energy Laboratory (NREL) officials always gave me a fair hearing, and often sought my opinion when they sensed I might want to share it. While it was easy to stew in frustration over an email exchange

or a multi-layered conference call, the reality of the complex challenges the DOE and NREL faced putting the event together became much more real when we arrived in Washington, and met the individuals face to face. It was much easier for us to make suggestions for improvements than it was for them to sort through suggestions from fourteen teams, and come to a fair and equitable solution. In this day and age of deepening cynicism about the role of government in society, it is incredible to me that such an extraordinary group of people can survive and even thrive while working for a vast government bureaucracy. It gives me hope that government really can have a positive impact.

[1] Energy Information Administration, www.eia.doe.gov

[2] U.S. Environmental Protection Agency, www.epa.gov

[3] ibid

[4] "Blueprint for the Clean, Sustainable Energy Age for the Protection of Health, Biosphere and Climate," *World Circle of the Consensus*, World Sustainable Energy Coalition, 2002.

[5] refer to various studies prepared for the U.S. Centers for Disease Control and Prevention; regarding student test score improvement, one of the best known studies is "Daylighting in Schools" completed in 1999 by the Heschong Mahone Group, www.h-m-g.com

[6] Aldo Leopold, *A Sand County Almanac, and Sketches Here and There*. New York: Oxford University Press, 1949, 1987.

[7] ibid

[8] ibid

[9] William McDonough and Michael Braungart, *Cradle to Cradle: Remaking the Way we Make Things*. New York: North Point Press, 2002.

[10] It is now an international competition. The 2005 Solar Decathlon includes teams from Spain and Canada.

Process

Design and build a house powered by solar energy no larger than 800 square feet. This was the primary challenge of the Solar Decathlon. On the surface, it sounds like the kind of assignment you could complete in a semester, with a summer for construction. Yet the complexity of the challenge required the concerted effort of over 100 students spread out over three and a half semesters and two summers. The design of the house was required to be:

- transportable to and from Washington DC
- a clear demonstration of the integration of renewable energy into a house
- sufficiently energy efficient to compete against other teams in a rigorous week of monitoring
- sophisticated enough to appeal to a jury of renowned architects
- innovative enough in architecture and engineering to meet the standards of our team
- completed on time, and within our budget (i.e. whatever amount we could fundraise)
- a worthy representative of our university and of our disciplines

Collaboration

To take on this contest, the students negotiated a complicated maze of ethical, aesthetic, technical and financial issues. The toughest situation an ecologically-minded designer faces is when circumstances threaten a design idea or a philosophical position. The challenge is compounded when the designer is not an individual, but a large group loosely organized as a democracy. Decisions that require careful consideration of trade-offs become more complex when they have to be made by a diverse team of people—each with their own experiences, interests and agendas. Decisions were sometimes fluid and dependent on the participants in the room at any given time.

The team collaborated on every aspect of the design process to resolve countless dilemmas and produce a self-sufficient, transportable house. In the process, they discovered there are few choices that are clearly right or wrong within design. Instead, they found themselves in a pluralistic process requiring great patience, tact, energy and honesty.

Throughout design and construction, the team was often embroiled in debates that occasionally threatened to dissolve a hard-won sense of collective decision-making. As the architecture faculty advisor, I anticipated the process of making design decisions as a team would be difficult. I was interested in testing a democratic, collective, and truly collaborative decision-making process, as a way to ensure every individual was truly invested in the project. I structured the first design studio so that everyone would have an equal hand in the design, but I didn't really believe equality was possible. I assumed one student's design would become the obvious choice, and we would move forward on that basis. Architectural education (and much of contemporary practice) is about the brilliant individual solving a problem on his or her own terms. Yet my initial assumption could not have been more wrong. To my surprise, it became clear that under certain conditions, design by committee is possible. More than anything, it takes a talented and mature group with the willingness to be both opinionated and open-minded.

Early in the sequence of the design studios and courses focused on the Solar Decathlon competition, architecture students began working with a small team of engineering students. As the architecture advisor, my goal was to help the architecture students learn how to collaborate with their engineering counterparts. Given their differing educations, it is not surprising that the students spoke different languages. As the engineers were talking about optimization and efficiency, the architects were more interested in ambiguity between building and landscape. While the engineers were trying to logically move in a linear fashion through a set of decisions, the architects were making great leaps forward and backward (and sideways). Taken to the logical extreme, the engineers' solution would have been an upgraded single-wide trailer with a lot of additional insulation, two small windows, and photovoltaic panels on the roof. For the architects, the most 'out there' scenario involved a building idea composed of a series of petals that opened and closed according to the season—vaguely resembling a multi-layered taco shell. Somewhere in the midst of the complex dialogue, the architects began to develop designs that the engineers could recognize as buildings, and the engineers became more open to the importance of spatial and conceptual ideas.

The engineers' willingness to blend into the late-night drafting culture of the architecture school was a major aspect of the early success of the project. Unfortunately, there were fewer opportunities for the architecture students to experience the atmosphere of the engineering school. (Engineers seldom work on building projects, and never in an open, public setting such as an architectural studio space.) The competition offered unique challenges as teacher. The engineering advisors and myself had to manage collaboration amongst our own students, and across the two disciplines. We could not waste a lot of time with unrealistic or unworkable solutions. I found myself constantly thinking of ways to encourage good decisions and clear communication. It was probably the toughest professional assignment I had ever faced.

During the early weeks of the first semester, I asked two things of the students. First, they were to measure themselves performing a domestic activity and create a drawing of this analysis. As they considered themselves sleeping, cooking, showering, dressing, etc., they became more aware of the scale of a human body. Next, I asked them to design an abstract fragment of a house in which to perform those activities. These fragments helped generate ideas later in the semester, and the kernel of some of those ideas even made it into the house's final design: one student's sensorial shower concept eventually became the bathroom; another student's fascination with adaptable dining tables and window frames led the team to design and build an adaptable rain screen panel system. In the final stages of detailing, the students ultimately figured out how to make the concept a reality by using reclaimed wood shipping palettes, all milled, cut and assembled into panels.

The next step was to analyze relevant architectural precedents, and to investigate engineering principles. The team researched passive design (shading, natural ventilation, thermal mass) and more technologically based renewable energies including photovoltaics, alternative daylighting, heating and cooling.

As the design process began in earnest, students worked in four teams of three, each team collaboratively creating twelve separate designs. The concepts, built as tiny 1/16" scale models, became collectively known as the "babies." Each baby was unique, and was born of a specific thesis or idea. After much discussion, each team discarded some of the babies and built the remainder at a larger scale. This often involved combining ideas from several babies, or using a baby as a jumping off point in a completely new direction. Eventually, the teams were asked to present one design to the group. I held a formal review at that stage, and invited the engineers to participate. Two engineering students consulted with each of the teams. After the comments, the entire group held a secret ballot, and the field of four was narrowed to two. The two "winning teams" were expanded, taking in the "losing" teams. The intention was to develop these two ideas further, but both houses were completely redesigned by the time of the next review, becoming more thoughtful and rigorous hybrids of the original four designs.

At the next review, another vote was held, and the final "winner" was selected. The design packed all the 'service' elements (plumbing, mechanical, kitchen, bathroom, storage) into a zone to the north of the house, leaving the remainder of the house open for living spaces. With the entire team now working on one design, it was inevitable that the house would continue to change. Ultimately, the floor plan from that stage in the project resembles the final built house, but the interior relationships and the articulation of the exterior form are significantly different. Throughout the semester, as the teams got larger, the designs became more sophisticated. Ideas that were hard to defend fell away, and good ideas were left behind.

Insurgency
Soon after the entire studio came together to work on one design a small insurgent group of students became dissatisfied with the rigid quality of the design, and late one night temporarily "took over" the design. I had assigned the studio a 1/2" section model of the building—a small slice. I had actually been assigning these models for a few weeks, but no one seemed to get around them. This time the insurgent group decided to take the 1/2" model requirement to the next level. Instead of building a small section, they built a 1" model

"These students not only worked with each other, but they worked with professionals from both fields who helped them along the way. This was a big, complex project that they had to carry through to completion. They had to build it, and it had to work. Along the way, they had to address all kinds of real-world issues that get left out of classroom situations—things like cost, materials comparison and selection, environmental considerations, safety issues around working with power tools and wearing hard hats, and project management. With 100 people working on the team, the time spent managing the different tasks and making sure that things came together properly was enormous."

Paxton Marshall, engineering advisor

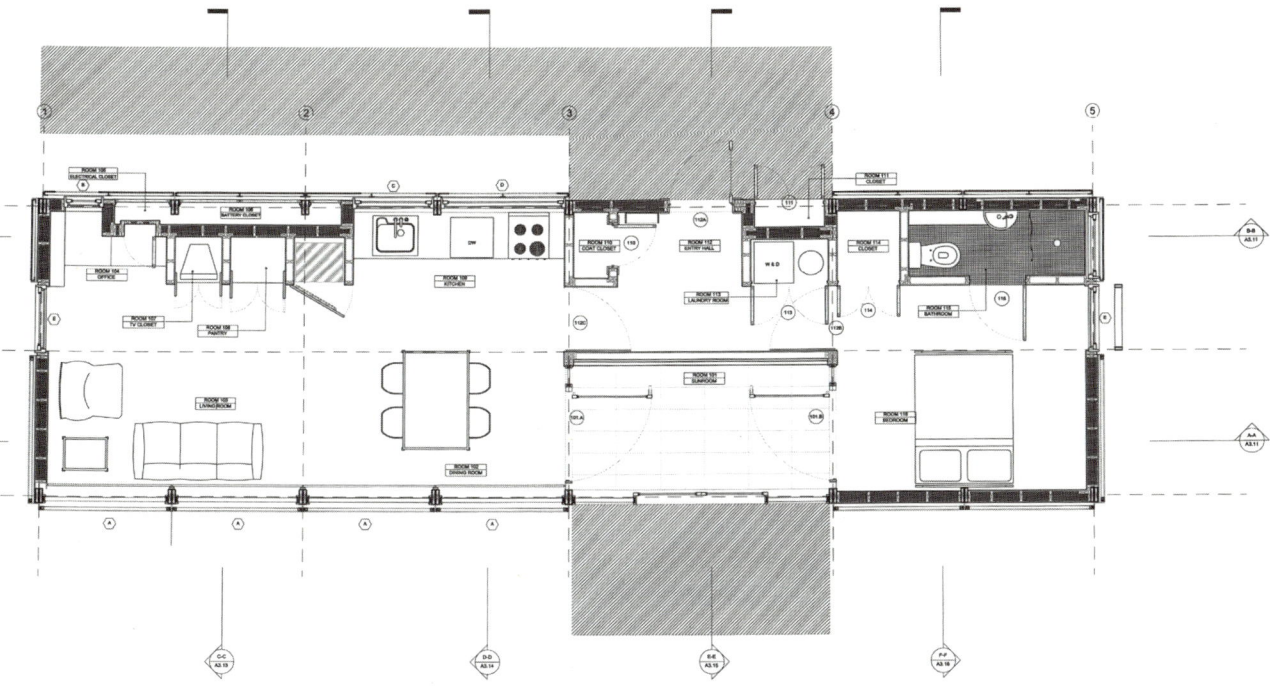

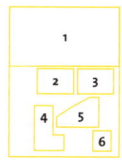

1
Floor plan

2
Architecture students Danny MacNelly, Adam Ruffin, Ben Spencer and Brian Gerich discuss design details

3
Computer rendering of interior to study light conditions

4
Early design study of the Trojan Goat taking on Washington, DC

5
Exploded axonometric drawing of rainscreen system

6
Corner detail study of rainscreen wall

of the entire building—but their interpretation of it. They used the same floor plan, but completely changed the exterior expression of the building—with hinged and sliding panels flying all over the place. The model was so quickly and poorly crafted that it was easy to dismiss. Yet it had a power—as well as a subtlety and spirit—that the "final" design lacked. During a long review and discussion, the studio came together and decided to incorporate many of the insurgents' ideas, but refine them, and to organize them into a rational system. It was painful and difficult, but everyone felt the building was going to be better for it. It also helped the students realize that they each had an equal voice in the project.

A Goat Ethic
At this critical stage in the project the house got its nickname. A student and I were talking about how the newly suggested sliding and hinging louvers and panels could form a climate responsive skin around the entire building. I said that it reminded me of the Trojan Horse, in the way the building could arrive with a mysterious wooden wrapper, and then unfold to reveal its true intentions. Another student had a long-standing and oft-stated obsession with goats, extremely adaptable and efficient animals that can survive on most any food. Similarly, we hoped our design would be adaptable. "Goat" had become an adjective for anything cool or interesting within the studio, and thus as we discussed the Trojan Horse, it almost immediately became the "Trojan Goat."

Several faculty and outside advisors questioned the use of this name, but I have always defended it. I believe it helps the original studio have some ownership over the final result. It seems to define the spirit of that first studio, and helped students who joined the project afterwards have a clearer understanding of the original intent.

The Trojan Goat identity clarified the ethical framework of the design. The students decided they wanted the building to be ecologically responsible, but on their own terms. It didn't need to be polite as much as clear about its intentions. It was to be like the animal it was named after: climate responsive; adaptable; resourceful; determined; intelligent; comfortable; highly evolved, but maybe a little rough around the edges. Hence the house was to be refined, but visibly handcrafted.

Toward the end of that first semester, it became clear to me that these values were even more important to the students than the form of the building they had designed. Each student had to give up on a design idea at some point in the collaborative process, which meant the building design was no longer precious or untouchable. They were headed for graduation, and knew another group of students would be taking the project through completion. They cared deeply about the building they had designed, but they were even more concerned about the ideas that helped determine its form. In an effort to smooth that transition, we had two long discussions about the development of a written document stating the ideas and goals of the project. Everyone had to agree on the content. More than making an aesthetic object, they wanted to elaborate an enduring Goat ethic.

Refinement

The next major challenge was to transfer the intentions of the original studio to another group of students. In the fall of 2001, I co-taught a construction detailing class with my engineering counterpart, Professor Paxton Marshall, and part-time Research Scientist, Dan Pearce. It was a conventional class (as opposed to a design studio), held in the architecture school, but with equal representation of architecture and engineering students. The architecture students were mostly graduate students, with a few undergraduate architecture and graduate landscape architecture students. The class was divided into inter-disciplinary groups, focused on specific topics, such as structural design, electrical controls, landscape design and daylighting. The students prepared presentations on their issues, and worked towards resolving the house design.

This course structure gave equal weight to architectural and engineering issues. Since neither group had a permanent studio space, our gathering place became the ethernet of the university's computer network. Email and a web-based class forum became our primary method of collaboration and communication outside of class time.

The challenges of inter-disciplinary collaboration, which had been an undercurrent all along, became a major source both of concern and inspiration. There were differing expectations about what a house should be. A few of the new engineering students were surprised by the unconventional look of the design. They could not understand why it was not similar to a typical single-wide trailer, which is easy to transport, easy to build, and if well insulated, can be energy efficient. The new architecture students had to defend a house designed by their predecessors. Rather than attempting to redesign the house, the architecture team became protective of both the building form and the ethical principles behind it. Fortunately, the design's well-proportioned module is simultaneously flexible and rigid, allowing for refinement of the interior spaces and exterior skin without a complete rethinking of the building form.

The process of questioning design decisions forced the new design team members to take a close look at the drawings and identify weaknesses and strengths. The engineering team expressed two major concerns: 1) the flat roof, and 2) the almost complete lack of insulation or solid wall along the south, east and west walls. The architecture team succeeded in defending the former, and the entire team found an effective compromise on the latter.

The flat (or more accurately, low-slope) roof was important to the architecture students for two reasons. First, it allowed occupation of the roof, with one quarter of its area set aside for a green roof. Since the house size was limited to 800 square feet (ours was actually 750), the designers wanted to "expand" the house by including the surrounding landscape, and making a direct connection between the built form and its "unbuilt" context. With plants growing both on and

"Projects like the Trojan Goat could change the way people occupy buildings. Understanding a smart home's technology, or the basic principles behind the technology, hopefully will lead to a higher awareness of the environment and environmental issues. The architects and engineers of tomorrow were given the opportunity to research sustainable materials and building practices, to put their green designs in place, and to work with energy-minded companies."

Charlotte Barrows, architecture project manager, undergraduate student next to the building, this relationship is clarified. Second, the flat roof maximizes the interior space of the house, which had a strict 18'-0" height restriction from the DOE. With sufficient floor and roof structure to travel on a federal interstate and a 9'-0" interior ceiling height in the main living spaces, there was not room to put in a conventional sloped roof, and to mount the photo-voltaic (PV) panels at the ideal angle. Therefore, the PVs had to fold down to fit under highway bridges. In addition, the team had decided to build the house as one structure (rather than several pieces that would be put together on site) and unless a separate gable was attached in place, a conventional pitched roof would carve into the clarity of the interior spaces by bringing the ceiling height down. The engineers were convinced.

As for the lack of solid walls, the architecture students did not deny the legitimacy of the engineering students' concerns. Full height glazing over half of all the vertical surfaces of the building is not the most energy-efficient way to enclose a house. Yet the original design intent was to maximize the ambiguity between inside and outside—and to critique the typical trailer-style impenetrable box. With a full-height glass wall, the occupants benefit from a more direct connection with the adjacent exterior space.

During the height of summer, heat gain would be significant, but the architecture team had already addressed this with a flexible, exterior skin—the sliding, hinged, louvered wood panels. In the final design, the panels could be adjusted to block all heat gain. However, the architecture students had not adequately addressed heat loss during winter. The ultimate solution was two-fold. The majority of the east and west walls, as well as the eastern-most quarter of the south wall (the bedroom) would become mostly solid and fully insulated. This arrangement had the added benefit of providing privacy. For the remainder of the south wall, the architecture team committed to a minimum thermal resistance factor (R-value) of 17. The engineering team agreed the architecture team could keep their full-height of glass on the south wall as long as they met the absolute minimum standard for thermal performance of a conventional solid wall. This was a major compromise on their part, as the thermal resistance for the remaining solid walls of the Trojan Goat is an unusually high R-35. The architecture team resolved this by finding a window company that makes high performance fiberglass frame windows (Comfortline) with an R-value of 10—very high for windows. They also designed a customized thermal curtain for the south windows with two layers of Thinsulate, an efficient and cost effective insulator. In the end, the R-value of the south wall is just under the R-17 goal—R-16.5 with the curtains pulled closed.

The resolution of the exterior wall insulation issue is the perfect example of the advantages of inter-disciplinary collaboration. The debate started with a question: "Why so many windows?" and a first response: "Because we want to make the walls disappear, and bring the outside in." It ended with the engineering team setting a performance standard that would work within their mechanical design assumptions, and with the architecture team refining and adjusting their original idea to meet this standard. The final result has a selec-

"When I was a fourth-year student, I interviewed with defense contractors and big builders, thinking I would get a job straight out of college. Then I worked on the solar house and decided to go to graduate school instead. Now, I want to work in solar and wind-powered fuel cells, which means I'll probably end up working for a much smaller firm—not a big corporation."

Dave Click, engineering project manager, undergraduate student

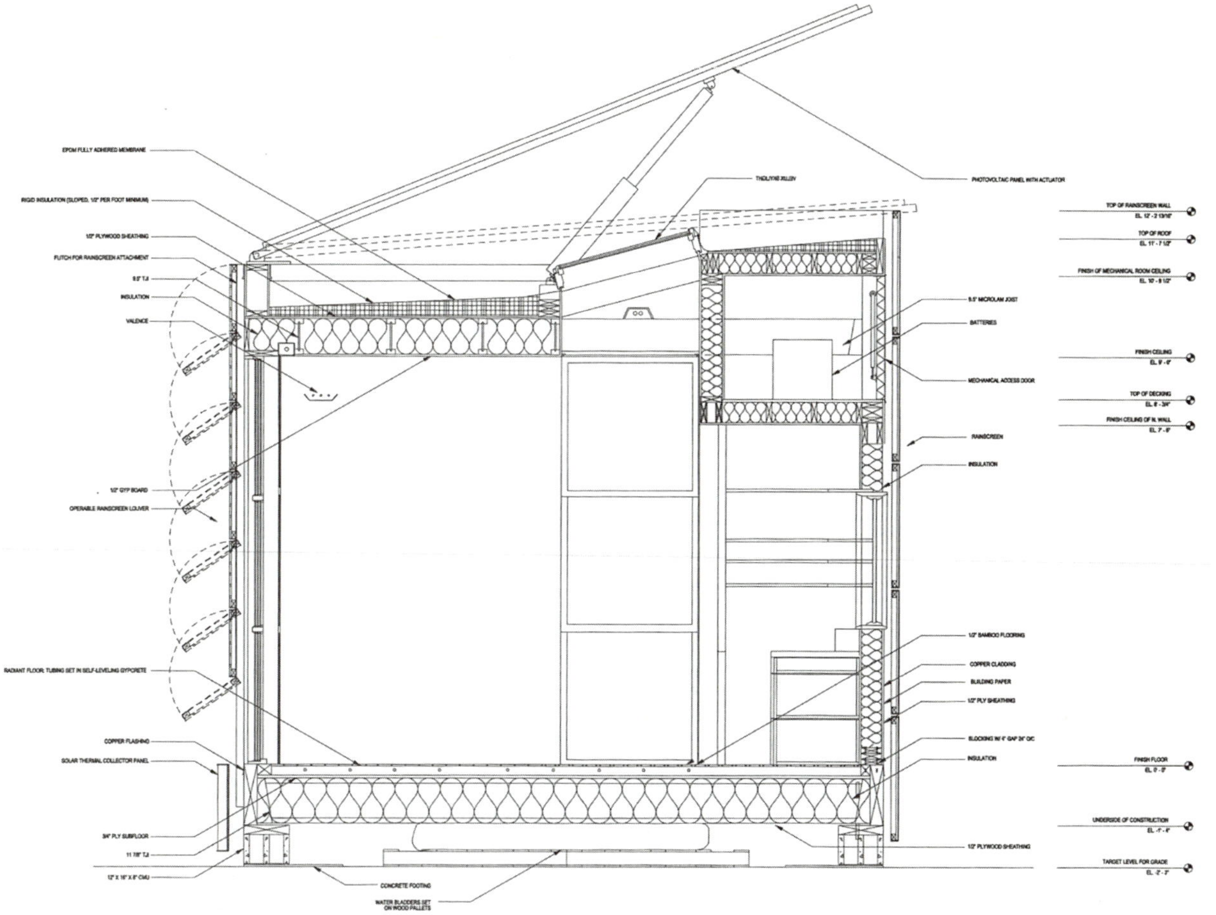

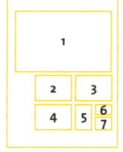

1
Building section

2
Construction begins with a demonstration of power tools

3
Sketch to locate reclaimed tire garden/ecosystems

4
Section detail of deck attachment

5
Architecture student Dawn Balsam participates in palette disassembly process

6
The final scale model of the building

7
Architecture student Scott McGihon rests during wood palette disassembly process

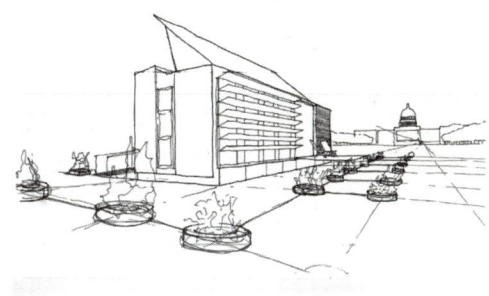
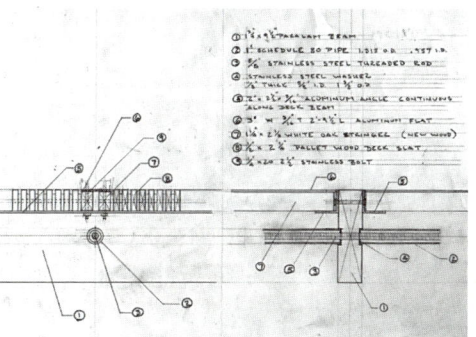

tive and tactical use of glazing, and a more thoughtful aesthetic. The engineers got their insulation, and the architects got their spatial continuity where it matters the most—in the living and dining room spaces. Aesthetics and ethics were balanced and intertwined.

It was during this second full semester that the team added landscape architecture students. Ideally, this would have occurred in the beginning, so that the dialogue between inside and outside would have equal voices. The small team of two graduate landscape architecture students formulated their own Goat ethic, and even considered bringing a live goat to chomp on the grass of the National Mall in Washington, DC. They established principles for design on both the site in Washington (a movable landscape, in every sense of the word) and the intended final resting place for the house on the grounds of the university. It was an upward battle for the first landscape team members, as they attempted to challenge the architecture, and work with engineering students, who were less than clear about the nature of landscape architecture.[1]

It was a difficult semester in many ways, but by the end of the semester, engineering students became protective of the building form. One even expressed concern about a minor change to the building section that would affect the proportions of the building. For their part, many of the architecture students were beginning to take seriously the ideas and issues expressed by the engineering team. They were looking for performance criteria in their material selection process, and reading up on dangers of air infiltration.

Resolution
In the spring of 2002, the architecture team expanded again with a second 4th year undergraduate studio, collaborating directly with graduate students participating in independent study. I started the studio with two simultaneous assignments:

1) the compilation of a thorough, collaborative progress report on the house design—with a candid assessment of the Trojan Goat's strengths and weaknesses, and
2) a small team collaborative design/build project—a small temporary shelter, to be assembled from reclaimed materials, set up in three hours, and occupied during a cold, winter night

These assignments allowed the new team members to become familiar with both the design of the Trojan Goat, and the underlying principles of passive design. To put together the report, the new students interviewed engineering, architecture and landscape architecture students from the previous semesters—only some of whom were continuing on. They collaborated on the opinions expressed, and compiled a coherent package. In the process of designing and building their small sleeping shelter, they learned about solar gain, insulation and thermal lag. Their understanding of these issues would have a direct impact on their own sleeping comfort. I organized the shelter project as a mini-Solar Decathlon, with winners being selected by a group of architecture and engineering students and professors. The criteria were Vitruvius' triad—firmness, commodity and delight.

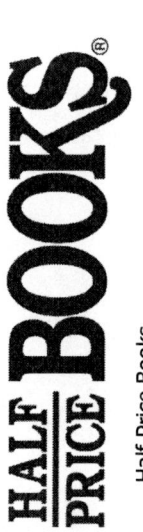

HALF PRICE BOOKS®

Thank you for your order, VINDY-BXC-StorePO22313825y-1!

Half Price Books
1835 Forms Drive
Carrollton, TX 75006
OFS OrderID   37353986

Thank you for shopping with Half Price Books! Please contact service96@hpb.com. if you have any questions, comments or concerns about your order (113-7744138-6423416)

SKU	ISBN/UPC	Title & Author/Artist	Shelf ID	Qty	OrderSKU
S430664798	9780977102402	Trojan Goat: A Self-Sufficent House (Winne… John D. Quale	HOM8.1	1	

ORDER# **113-7744138-6423416**
AmazonMarketplaceUS

SHIPPED STANDARD TO:
VINDY-BXC-StorePO22313825y-1
35 SW 12th Avenue, Ste 102
22313825-Y
Dania Beach FL 33004
sj7j4k2yw5fhlwn@marketplace.amazon.com

The design process had been underway for over a year before this new group of students came on board, and yet each of them became intimately involved in the final resolution of the design. They were assigned tasks, based on their interests—from window and door design to rain screen wall detailing; and from bathroom refinement to cabinetry design. They had to collaborate with team members that (initially) knew the house better than they did, and work within constraints that sometimes appeared capricious. Yet their work, in combination with the engineering and independent study architecture students, made the final construction possible. They put together a coherent set of construction drawings. They researched environmental materials; resolved the placement of mechanical, plumbing and electrical systems with the engineering team; set standards for the refinement of the cabinetry; and made a definitive 3-D computer model. They respected their predecessors' ideas and overall strategy, and still found a way to make the building their own.

At some point during the previous fall, the architecture team decided to design and build as much of the furniture and cabinetry in the house as possible. Architecture professor Theo Van Groll, who taught a furniture course in the school for many years, agreed to let the Trojan Goat become the focus of his spring class. Obviously, this complicated matters, as there were an additional thirteen students involved, most of whom knew little about the Trojan Goat design. Yet the group built several thoughtfully designed and carefully crafted pieces. During the event in Washington, visitors were surprised to learn that the cabinetry and furniture were designed and built by students.

Conflict

As summer approached, many students were itching to get their hands dirty, and to start building. After a long process to refine, verify and finalize the structural design, we were ready to place an order for lumber. The team had elected to use composite wood joists and framing—commonly known as engineered lumber. As opposed to steel framing, which would require professional welding, the use of engineered lumber made it possible for even the most inexperienced team members to participate in the framing process. The lumber is not cut from solid tree trunks, but instead utilizes smaller shreds and shards of wood, pressed and formed together with adhesives. Compared with standard lumber, engineered lumber is stronger, and is generally perceived as a more ecological product due to the use of wood material that might otherwise be considered scrap. However, some environmentalists, architects and engineers question the environmental impact of the adhesives. The team researched the issue carefully and decided the benefits outweighed the disadvantages. Weyerhaeuser–Trus Joist agreed to donate all the joists and framing members, and also helped us verify our structural assumptions and calculations. We sent them a list of products, and waited for the order to arrive. On the day of the first delivery, an error on Weyerhaeuser's part sparked the most heated and interesting debate of the entire project.

The house rests on two 4" x 16" x 48'-0" beams along the bottom of the south and north walls of the building. They carry all the live and dead loads, and are connected to two other beams on the east and

"Really, we're trying to change every convention that anyone has about how you build a house, how you power that house, how your house actually operates when you are there and not there, how you relate to it, how it relates to everything else."

Adam Ruffin, architecture project manager, graduate student

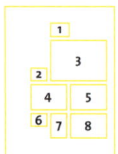

1
Architecture students
Adam Ruffin and Alex Butler
move pressure treated
perimeter beams

2
Architecture wood shop manager Dave Williams and architecture student Kirk Jansen
assemble interior cabinetry

3
Floor framing is complete

4
Architecture students Adam
Ruffin and Bolanle Adeboye
cutting lumber

5
Architecture student
Danny MacNelly framing
the south wall

6
Engineering project manager
Ben Dorrier and engineering
advisor Dan Pearce begin the
process of attaching the
photovoltaics to the roof

7
Construction volunteer assists
with assembling the solar
hot water panels

8
Installing the aluminum
frames for the south
wall louvers

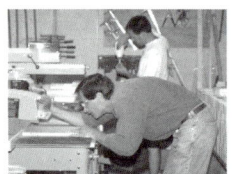

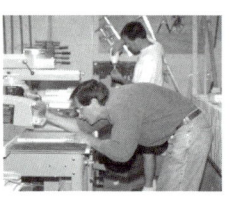

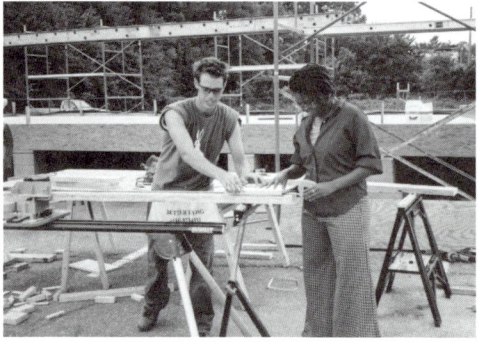

west walls. After careful consideration by several graduate architecture students it was decided to specify non-pressure treated lumber. In locations where wood might be directly exposed to moisture, lumber (both conventional and engineered) is typically treated under high pressure with a toxic recipe of chemicals. At the time, the most common method of pressure treatment, known as CCA, included arsenic, and was under careful review by the U.S. Environmental Protection Agency. It has since been outlawed for use in single-family homes, playground equipment and child care centers. This is based on evidence that arsenic and other chemicals leach into the ground, and that the material is potentially dangerous to handle—particularly during the construction process.

Our Weyerhaeuser representative mistakenly assumed we wanted pressure treated lumber for the perimeter beams. When the lumber arrived, we had to decide whether to use the material, or ask that it be replaced. If we had purchased the material, it would have been a non-issue —we would simply return it. But since it was donated, we could not easily ask Weyerhaeuser to exchange the order.

I sent an email to the team asking if we should use the pressure treated beams, or send them back. We could offer to pay for the new material, or at least the shipping costs. We couldn't really afford to pay for anything that would otherwise be donated, and we certainly didn't want to offend our donors. We had just submitted a grant proposal to the Weyerhaeuser Foundation requesting additional funding for the project, making the political quandary more complex. For over two weeks the emails flew back and forth, breaking largely into four overlapping camps: 1) those who wanted to use the material even if it wasn't ideal; 2) those who felt untreated engineered lumber should never have been considered; 3) those who felt the environmental concerns outweighed the technical and financial issues and wanted to buy the new material; and 4) those who wanted to get Weyerhaeuser to replace the material at no cost. Passionate emails quoted dense EPA reports on CCA; articles from *Fine Homebuilding* and *Environmental Building News* about the subject; and personal experiences about working with pressure treated lumber.

In the end, we reached an elegant compromise. We elected to keep the pre-cut short beam pieces, as they could not be used by anyone else, and might otherwise end up in the waste stream. I successfully convinced Weyerhaeuser to replace and restock the two long CCA treated beams with untreated beams. To address the potential of arsenic leaching from the treated beams, and the concern about moisture with the untreated beams, the team researched and purchased "environmentally responsible" sealants and finishes. One of the treated beams was encased in a durable sealer, and the other left exposed. Ferns which are known to remove arsenic from soil—a form of phyto-remediation—will eventually be planted adjacent to the exposed, treated beam. As for the untreated beams, one was painted with a durable, opaque finish, and the other beam received a transparent finish that will need to be renewed every few years. Each of the products selected is considered ecologically benign, with little or no off-gassing from volatile organic compounds. In short, the Trojan Goat became a living laboratory for research on alternatives to pressure treatment and methods of mediating the effects of CCA.

Construction began in a Crozet, Virginia asphalt parking lot during an unusually hot and humid summer. The parking lot was on loan from a local developer who also owned several neighboring industrial buildings—including a former frozen food plant. The closest neighboring building was filled with frozen turkeys that summer. Several 'goats' dreamed of visiting the turkeys on the hottest days.[2]

New people continued to join the team—both students and members of the local community. Several of them became so integral to the project that it became hard to imagine how we could have completed the project without them. One student devoted her entire summer and most of the fall to working on the project, after showing up to see if she might help for a couple hours. Two students from the very first semester—one engineering and one architecture—rejoined the team in the last month or so.

The design continued to simplify and change as funding ran low, and the students realized the complexity of some of the design ideas. They learned it is often easier to draw than to build.

Migration

The process of getting the house to Washington had long been a topic of research and design. Although the building was built to be mobile, it could not move in the same way as a manufactured or modular home. The Trojan Goat was informed by the team's design ideas and optimized for the DOE design guidelines—neither of which lent itself to the building proportions of conventional manufactured housing. In the end, the Virginia Department of Transportation deemed the house a 'super load'—too long, too wide, too tall and too heavy to travel under a normal modular house permit. We employed the services of two companies to help us transport it—a regional house moving company to lift and lower the house in Crozet and Washington onto a trailer provided by a national heavy hauling company. Built on a series of concrete pads—far enough apart to allow the 'low-boy' trailer to back under the house when it was lifted with hydraulic jacks, the 86,000 pound house fit perfectly on a trailer bed. Once strapped in place, the professional driver carefully maneuvered the house out of the frozen turkey plant parking lot late one night to the cheers of the team as well as several local residents watching from their front porches and windows. A couple of students and I traveled behind the Goat all the way to Washington, at speeds up to 65 miles an hour. The truck made a scheduled overnight stay in Northern Virginia (to give us some flexible time, in case something went wrong), so it could cross into Washington, DC after dark, and begin to tear up the well groomed lawn of the National Mall in front of the Smithsonian museums at precisely 12:01 AM the next morning. The organizers had carefully planned the arrival sequence—like an awkward ballet for oversized boxes.

It was our first chance to see the houses from the other universities. After two years figuring out our own design, it was exciting to see the products of other teams, and how they approached the same challenge. The designs ranged from a very well built, but mostly conventional trailer home (with a lot of very nice upgrades) from Crowder College, a small two-year institution, to a high-tech fiberglass and glass box from our neighbor (in the state, and on the National Mall) Virginia Tech. One favorite of mine was the elaborate

component based modular design from the University of Texas at Austin. They had designed and fabricated a series of modular parts and pieces that arrived in semi-trailers. That first night, the only aspects visible of their design were neatly stacked piles of structural and panelized pieces. During the first week of the competition, as we were to complete the final assembly of the house, the form of the UT-A house emerged and was attached to a nicely renovated Airstream trailer, housing the kitchen and other plumbing elements.

The Final Push
Meanwhile, our house was supposed to arrive in one piece, allowing the Trojan Goat warriors to simply sit in lawn chairs and watch the rest of the teams; but in reality, we were a little behind schedule. The house was fully enclosed, and had most of the exterior and interior fittings in place. But things always take longer than you think they will, and we had a long list of small tasks to complete.

We kept up a frantic pace that last week—working well into the night. The Marriott hotel chain put us up in hotel just across the Potomac River, but we seldom saw it that first week. On the last night before the first public viewing, the entire team stayed up all night one last time, and 'finished' the house. I have two striking memories from that night—one was working with a student to sand and finish the bamboo floor with a palm sander (as nothing else was available); the other was the sense that in the waning hours of work, distinctions between architecture, engineering and landscape architecture students entirely disappeared. The students knew each other so well at that point, that the final push seemed like a carefully choreographed performance. Team members were effortlessly trading tools, finding lost drill bits and stepping over each other as if they could anticipate everyone else's moves.

The next morning, as the public began to arrive, and several members of the team awoke from naps in the back deck, no one was prepared to share the newly completed Goat just yet. We wanted to pause and appreciate our two years of work, yet the public arrived by the thousands. The DOE estimates that well over 100,000 people visited the "solar village" during the official public days, with over

400,000 hits on the Solar Decathlon website each day of the event. Lines soon formed to tour the houses, and the team quickly became tour guides. We had many questions about the copper cladding, but mostly people said they loved the house. More accurately, many prefaced their comments with something like "I was a little hesitant about your house from the outside, but...." Many noted the bright, spacious feel of the interior, and more than a few were convinced the house had to be more than 750 square feet.

The team leaders and advisors met with DOE and NREL officials daily throughout the event. The organizers were busy trying to balance the demands of the teams, the media that swarmed the event, and the many government officials and politicians that visited. The NBC-TV *Today Show* did a few live remotes. Members of our team were interviewed by the *New York Times*, the *Washington Post*, *Parade Magazine*, *Architecture Magazine*, National Public Radio's *Weekend Edition*, HGTV, and the DIY Network, among many others.

The first event was the judging of the Design and Livability event— the architecture category. The judges included Steve Badanes, Dr. Douglas Balcomb, Dr. Ed Jackson, Jr., Edward Mazria, Glenn Murcutt, and Stephanie Vierra. They visited each house and spoke with the team. When the winners were slowly announced, we kept expecting to hear our team. We had almost given up when Glenn Murcutt announced that we won First Place. The judges spoke highly of the project. Murcutt said, "There was little question that Virginia had the most inspired house." It was a very proud moment for everyone on the team, and made all the hard work seem worthwhile. We learned later it was a unanimous decision.

A few other teams were disappointed with our success in the architecture category. They complained to DOE and NREL officials we had ignored a vague reference in the rules to "consumer acceptance." Our contemporary design was at odds with what some participants felt was acceptable for the general public. Some teams were guided by those words and intentionally designed homes that looked exactly like a typical suburban ranch house. The teams specifically requested that the DOE organize a vote of the public to determine "public acceptance."

"When I think back on the Goat, I am amazed at what we were able to accomplish. I currently work as an assistant project manager for a construction company doing tenant build-outs and now deal, on a daily basis, with all of the same issues we struggled with during design and construction. The fact that such an inexperienced team, in design, construction, and project management, was able to come together and accomplish what we did speaks to the passion we all brought to the table. We all had varying ideas, some very far apart, but we were able to make it all work because we believed in the principals we were trying to demonstrate. All of the architects and engineers involved left the project with a huge head start in the direction the whole construction industry is going. Beyond what I learned about the architecture and engineering of a solar house, the overall process was a great segue from college into the professional world."

Ben Dorrier, engineering project manager, undergraduate student

The votes had no impact on the overall outcome of the competition, but ballots were made available at the information stands on the Mall. Although we were firmly committed to our design, and to "public acceptance" on our own terms, we were frustrated that the organizers agreed to hold the ballot largely in response to our design. The public voted over several days, and in the end, the results were pretty similar to the architecture judges. There was one major change—UVA finished in third place in the public ballot, and Crowder College, who failed to make the top five in the official category, took first place.

A problem with the control of our hot water systems and a broken dishwasher presented challenges for us in a few of the nine other (mostly engineering-based) events. The engineering students spent most of the fully monitored week running up and down ladders to the mechanical spaces (which the architecture students had insisted were the best place for them...) tinkering with the system. Eventually gaining control of the systems, and with the use of a borrowed dishwasher, we slowly began to work our way back from Ninth Place (our lowest ranking, despite our First Place in design). By the end of the week, everything was working smoothly. On the last day, we were amazed to learn we came in Second Place overall, not far behind the team from the University of Colorado at Boulder.

After two challenging years of inter- and intra-disciplinary collaboration with an incredible group of students, the comment that especially pleased me was that of architecture jury chairwoman Stephanie Vierra: "The UVA team attempted to integrate more solar strategies and did it more successfully than any other team. The work of the architecture and engineering students complemented each other in a way that set them apart from the other teams."

Final note: In addition to the First Place finish in architecture, and Second Place overall, the UVA team tied for First Place in the Energy Balance category, was awarded a special citation from the American Institute of Architects, and received the BP Solar "Progressive Award" for the most forward-thinking team. In 2003, the UVA team's website received an Honor Award in the student category of 2003 Entablature Website Design Awards. Paxton Marshall's engineering students con-

tinued to tinker with the systems after the house returned to Virginia. All the systems have been monitored, and several students have prepared a thesis based on their research.

After several attempts to find a permanent home for the Trojan Goat, I eventually negotiated with UVA officials to donate it to Piedmont Housing Alliance (PHA), a Charlottesville non-profit housing organization. As of this writing, PHA is preparing to sell the house to raise funds for their low-income housing programs.

I am currently working with PHA on another student design/build effort—ecoMOD—focused on ecological, modular and affordable houses. The project poses much more complex site and financial challenges, but we have the opportunity to set our own guidelines. I'm working again with Paxton Marshall, who is managing the engineering students. A minimum of three houses will be completed over the next several years, and each of them will be carefully analyzed prior to the design of the following one. We will monitor the building systems, assess the landscape, generate a life cycle analysis of the materials and construction methods, and complete a market analysis with the help of business students. More information is available on that project at www.ecomod.virginia.edu.

[1] The exposure to landscape architecture must have had some impact on the engineering students. One of the engineers from that semester eventually pursued a master of landscape architecture degree at UVA, finishing up in 2005.

[2] To continue the animal analogy, during the summer of 2005, the Trojan Goat temporarily moved to another parking lot—owned by the local Moose lodge. The Goat visited the Moose as it was being prepared for sale.

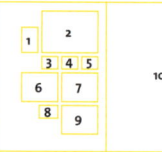

1
Engineering advisor Paxton Marshall tests battery of electric car for "Getting Around" contest

2
The Trojan Goat is lowered on to an oversize lowboy trailer with the assistance of the team from Virginia House Movers

3
The public days of the event attracted over 100,000 visitors to the National Mall

4
Southwest corner

5
West elevation

6
Architecture project manager Charlotte Barrows leads tours of the interior of the Trojan Goat

7
Engineering student Martin Miller after the last all-nighter to complete the building

8
Engineering students tinker with the mechanical systems during monitored phase of the competition

9
Engineering and architecture students recover from one more all-nighter to finish the construction of the house

10
Lines form in front of the Trojan Goat on the public viewing days of the competition

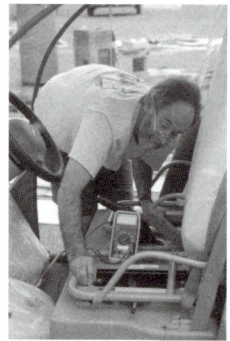

Product

Sunspace

Materials: reclaimed bluestone, paving pedestals, steel clips for stone attachment

The sunspace serves as both an exterior and an interior space, depending on the season. Opening and closing a series of sliding and hinging doors can change its relationship to the outdoors, allowing it to serve as a terrace during the summer and an enclosed solar heat gain space during the winter. Oriented to the south, the sunspace can be shaded with a sliding panel to block solar gain or left exposed to collect heat. The thermal mass of the dark stone holds heat, which can be drawn into the house with miniature fans located in the air space behind the stone wall. The bluestone on the floor and wall of the sunspace is reclaimed from a terrace renovation at the Rotunda at the University of Virginia, designed by Thomas Jefferson. The team designed the pattern of the stone, and cut it themselves. The stones are not only efficient as thermal mass, but embody the team's philosophy of material reuse.

Green Roof

Materials: green roof system, plantings, soil, stone

The Trojan Goat traveled with its own landscape. One quarter of the roof is comprised of a green or planted roof. The roofing membrane, provided by American Hydrotech, keeps the water out, while providing sufficient drainage for the plants. Draught resistant plants, such as sedums, keep the area green throughout much of the year. The green roof measures only ten by twelve feet, yet it serves as an inhabitable garden, a storm water reservoir, a producer of oxygen, and an insulator of the house.

Rainscreen

Materials: red and white oak lumber reclaimed from shipping palettes, aluminum frame

A rainscreen is an extra layer of weather protection to minimize the extremes of heat, cold and moisture on an exterior wall. The Trojan Goat's rainscreen is a porous layer of slatted wall panels, deflecting cold winds, shading from the hot sun and keeping most of the precipitation away from the copper siding beneath. The panels transform a waste product into an exterior skin. Wood shipping palettes were disassembled, planed and milled into usable lumber, and assembled into custom panels. The rain screen also embodies the conceptual basis of the Trojan Goat. The house arrives on site as a mysterious and closed box, like the Trojan Horse. The real intents of the building are revealed when the rain screen panels open and transform into decks, louvers, and window shades. Like the highly adaptable and resourceful goat, the rain screen allows the house to adapt to any site, and a variety of climatic conditions.

Copper Siding

Materials: reclaimed copper roofing

Beneath the rainscreen, the house is sheathed with copper siding reclaimed from the demolition of a roof installation. In using construction waste of local contractors, we diverted it from the scrap yard. The standing seam roofing had to be pulled apart, and the edges hammered flat. Once flattened, the copper was bent again to a new interlocking horizon lap detail appropriate for wall siding. Copper is durable, corrosion-resistant and recyclable.

Structure

Materials: engineered lumber, connectors
The structure of the Trojan Goat incorporates engineered lumber, a product that optimizes wood fiber utilization, thereby reducing waste and the deforestation rate. Composed of laminated or compressed layers of wood, engineered lumber can replace standard uses of wood and is stronger than pine or spruce members. Weyerhaeuser provided the engineered lumber products for the house. Simpson Strong Tie provided the connectors and fasteners, as well as three prefabricated "sheer walls," which we integrated into the north part of our structural frame.

To ensure the walls' maximum R-value, the engineered lumber was assembled using staggered-stud construction, offsetting every other 2 x 4 stud in a 2 x 6 wall. In doing so, thermal bridging was eliminated between interior and exterior surfaces, improving the insulative efficiency of the wall.

Insulation

Materials: spray-applied polyurethane foam insulation, blue-board insulation with IR reflective coating
The house's insulation is a spray-applied polyurethane foam installed by Creative Conservation of Richmond, Virginia and provided by Comfort Foam. Comfort Foam has an R-value of 7 per inch, the highest of all readily available, cost-effective insulations on the market. The walls of the Trojan Goat range from R-33 to R-70, significantly higher than a conventional wall with batt insulation. HCFC's have been largely removed from the process but not completely. Since the foam is a closed-cell system, it eliminates air infiltration. Although staggered studs reduced the conduction of heat through thermal bridging, at some locations thermal bridging could not be avoided. To resolve the matter, the walls have a second layer of insulation outside of the plywood sheathing. This layer is composed of 3/4" rigid board insulation that adds R-5. The foil layer on the outside of the board reflects heat, helping to keep the house cool in the summer.

Interiors

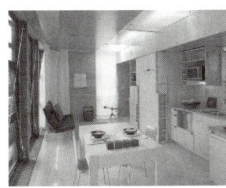

Materials: birch-veneer plywood, bamboo flooring, custom curtains with Thinsulate batting, glass tile
Wood is the dominant interior finish of the house. The ceiling and walls are lined with birch-veneer plywood, a material containing layers of wood that are rolled from a tree, rather than cut; the process yields more product and reduces waste. The layers are bonded with a resin adhesive and veneered with a high-quality face. The floor is finished with bamboo, a cost-effective alternative to wood flooring. Bamboo grass matures in three to five years, and its strength is comparable to red oak.

The living and dining room windows and the bedroom's large glass door are lined with a custom curtain made with two interior layers of Thinsulate. The curtain adds needed insulation to the large southern windows, and is also translucent, allowing light in during the day, but retaining complete privacy.

The bathroom is clad entirely in translucent, recycled glass tile. On one wall, the tile is installed over a large sheet of glass, which is placed a few inches inside of an operable exterior window. This detail allows for a continuous tile surface, and a large area of glowing natural light. At night the same area glows from an artifical light hidden in a slot, and is accessible only from outside the window.

Smartwall

Materials: light emitting diodes (LEDs), tablet PC, glass panels

Smartwall is a prototype for a new method of understanding, interacting with, and controlling the energy efficiency of a house. The wall glows different colors to indicate the temperature of the house—red when warm, blue when cool. The wall also provides information in the touch screen computer interface. The touch screen allows the inhabitant to interact with the house's control system via the internet. It provides real time readings of the temperature, humidity, power usage, battery storage, photovoltaic efficiency, and other metrics, and allows one to adjust various parts of the house to control the environment.

Landscape

Materials: reclaimed car tires, wire mesh baskets, soaker hoses, and vegetables

Linked to the green roof via a water collection system, the landscape at ground level, a "permanent landscape" for a movable solar house, posed a unique challenge. The Trojan Goat lived on the Mall in Washington, D.C. for three weeks and then returned to Charlottesville. Due to the house's itinerant nature, its landscape was represented in DC as a series of adaptable concepts for any location. The cisterns collect rainwater for irrigating the garden and flushing the toilet, and in turn the garden provides vegetables for the home. Like the house, the landscape attempts to transform waste into a resource. The tire planters are microclimates tempered by the soaker hoses that wrap them. Custom wire mesh baskets inserted in the tires separate the plant material from the tires, and allow for easy transplantation and transportion of plants. The organic vegetables grown in the planters were consumed as part of the required meal preparation aspect of the competition.

Luminaire

Materials: mirrored dish, solar tracker, glass fiber-optics

The house makes use of the world's first residential luminaire. Working with the Oak Ridge National Laboratory, architecture student Ben Spencer built a domestic scale version of an emerging technology that provides natural daylight at locations far from a window. A mirror dish on the roof of the house tracks the sun, and concentrates it into a polished glass fiber cable to deliver the natural light directly into the house's bathroom and entry hall. The glass fiber is attached to an etched glass tube in the entry and bathroom. The texture of the etching makes the light glow. In the future, electrical lights could be attached to the dish of the luminaire, to mimic natural light after the sun goes down.

Photovoltaics

Materials: silicon, aluminum

Electricity is produced by a rooftop photovoltaic (PV) array, consisting of sixteen 330-watt PV panels produced by ASE Americas. The PVs are connected to produce a 24-volt DC output. Excess electricity is stored in a bank of sealed Concord AGM lead-acid batteries. Additional energy is stored in the battery of the electric car, required for the "Getting Around" contest. A few of our loads, such as the refrigerator, ran directly off the DC supply, but most of the electric power is converted to 120-volt ac by two Trace electronic inverters.

Daylighting
Materials: windows, glass doors, skylights, sunlight

Natural light is used to illuminate the interior spaces in lieu of electrical lighting when possible. This method reduced the electrical load and produced a more natural interior environment. Daylight is delivered through a series of skylights, as well as through a strategically placed opening on each wall. Finally, a fiber optic luminaire transmits sunlight through a bundle of fiber optic cables, bringing it to specific areas for task lighting.

Cabinetry
Materials: birch veneer plywood, sustainably forested (FSC certified) maple butcher block countertop and desktop, plexiglass, aluminum, hardware

The cabinetry is composed of a limited palette of materials, chosen for economy and workability. The team designed the cabinetry as a single plane that is punctured at varying scales—maintaining the appearance of a single mass, while allowing for carefully composed flexibility. The design integrates storage and appliances, while maintaining flexibility for future uses.

Furniture
Materials: maple and cypress lumber, all sustainably forested (FSC certified), birch veneer plywood, hardware

The furniture was designed and built by students in architecture professor Theo van Groll's Architectural Crafts class. The students used sustainably forested lumber to build a platform bed with integrated storage base, a kitchen table with silverware drawers and a foldable deck chair.

Mechanical Systems
Materials: equipment, plumbing, water, air

The Trojan Goat heating and cooling systems are silent, energy efficient, ductless and draftless. These characteristics are important to the livability and comfort of the house, while they also reduce electrical loads compared to a forced air system. The heating of the house is achieved with passive solar design complemented by a radiant floor. This system utilizes water heated by solar thermal collector panels and can be supplemented by hot water from a geothermal heat pump.

Likewise, the house utilizes passive cooling methods, including shading and natural ventilation. When natural ventilation isn't sufficient, the heat pump chills water to cool and to dehumidify the house through a valance cooling unit located along the south edge of the ceiling in the dining area and in the bedroom. The valance is similar to a radiator heating system, except the fluid is cold. Condensation that forms on the piping is drained to the exterior with a simple metal gutter.

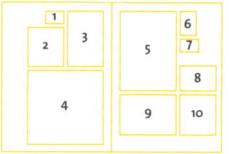

1
Architecture student Brian Gerich cuts stone for the sunspace

2
Bluestone reclaimed from paving at the UVA Rotunda

3
Stone reclaimed from the Rotunda at UVA, designed by Thomas Jefferson, was used to clad the walls of the sunspace

4
Assembly of deck panels

5
Copper siding

6
Installation of reclaimed copper siding

7
Architecture and landscape architecture student Jeff Aten hammers out reclaimed copper roofing

8
Construction of mechanical and electrical spaces on outside of north wall

9
Flooring framing completed

10
Copper siding

"Absolutely fantastic. This design encourages the public to move forward with integrating architecture and technology. Good mix of natural and electric lighting. Most innovative and pleasant living space. Very efficient floor plan. The team thought carefully about how the landscaping enhanced the house design."

Combined comments of the architecture jury

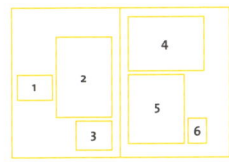

1
Shipping palettes are donated by Lowe's Home Improvement

2
The sunspace is the primary passive heat gain space of the house

3
The louver panels are adjusted with the flip of a switch

4
The rainscreen makes an adjustable, climate responsive skin for the Trojan Goat

5
The bedroom adjoins the sunspace to take maximum advantage of light and ventilation

6
The frame is structured to withstand the lateral forces the house will experience traveling down the road

53

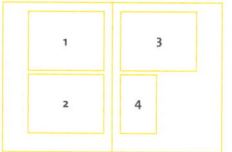

1
The open floor plan allows of overlapping activities between rooms

2
Natural finish woods provide the majority of interior finishes

3
The bathroom interior includes a sink, shower and toilet, and is clad in recycled glass tile

4
The cabinetry throughout the house is composed of a series of overlapping notched panels, allowing the utilization of every square inch of space

"University of Virginia group won the design and livability category—which measured innovation and aesthetics—with sensuous copper and wood cladding, rooftop photovoltaics, and an elegant design. In devising a climate-responsive house, the team seized on the idea of a hard exterior unfolding to reveal a highly refined, nicely detailed interior."

Kira L. Gould, *Metropolis* Magazine, January 2003

"In addition to its technical and experiential qualities, there is an element of delight in the UVA house that I would describe as déjà vu. You instantly know it works because even though it's new, it feels comfortable and familiar. The balance of mass and openness, light and shadow, texture and pattern creates a rhythm. The sense of delight gels as soon as you walk in and see that the technology does not get in the way of the communication between inside and out."

Dr. Ed Jackson Jr., architecture jury member

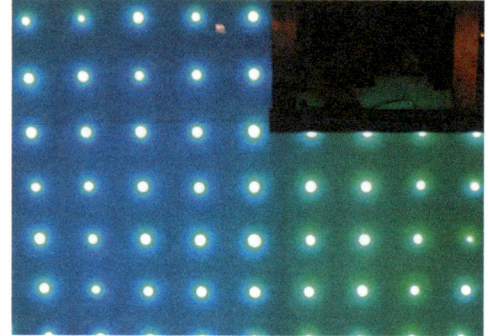

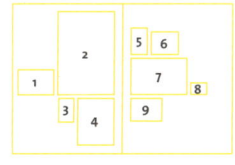

1
LED lights shine blue with the temperature of the house falls below the target temperature

2
Installation of bamboo flooring and birch veneer panels

3
The luminaire delivers natural light to the entry on the north side of the building

4
The entry hallway showing the Smartwall

5
Roof water is collected in two stainless steel cisterns attached to the side of the house

6
The green roof is designed and detailed by architecture student Joshua Galloway

7
The soaker hoses provide a continuous level of moisture to the soil, without wasting water

8
Engineering student Tyson Baldridge and architecture student Samantha Beadel tend to the green roof

9
A green roof occupies 25% of the Trojan Goat's roof area

UVA Solar Decathlon Team

1
The first team of architecture and engineering students measure out 800 square feet on the National Mall

Project Management Team

Students:

Adam Ruffin,
Master of Architecture,
May 2002, School
of Architecture

Dave Click,
Master of Science in
Electrical Engineering,
May 2003, School of
Engineering and
Applied Science

Charlotte Barrows,
Bachelor of Science in
Architecture, May 2002,
School of Architecture

Josh Dannenberg,
Bachelor of Science in
Architecture, May 2002,
School of Architecture

Ben Dorrier,
Bachelor of Science in
Mechanical Engineering,
December 2002, School
of Engineering and
Applied Science

Tim Sweeney,
Bachelor of Science in
Electrical Engineering,
May 2003, School of
Engineering and
Applied Science

Faculty:

John Quale,
Assistant Professor, School
of Architecture,
architecture advisor

Paxton Marshall,
Professor and Associate
Dean for Undergraduate
Affairs, School of
Engineering and
Applied Science,
engineering advisor

Dan Pearce,
Research Scientist,
School of Engineering
and Applied Science,
engineering advisor

Spring 2001
Schematic Design

*School of Architecture
Students (Arch 402
Architectural Design–
Sun Studio1):*

Bolanle Adeboye, Stephen
Allen, Peter DePasquale,
Kristi Dykema, Carmel
Greer, Jennifer Hall,
Stewart Hawkins, Aki
Hiltunen, Laura Landon,
Susan Meissner, Kate
Snider, Faye Whittemore

*School of Engineering and
Applied Science Students
(ECE 408 Electrical
Engineering Projects):*

Tyson Baldridge, Dave
Click, John Eterno,
Shannon Graeber, Jessica
McGowan, Jae Pak, Dan
Podhajny, Tim Sweeney

Summer 2001
Design Development

*School of
Architecture Students:*

Peter DePasquale, Laura
Landon, Kate Snider

*School of Engineering and
Applied Science Students:*

John Eterno,
Dan Podhajny, Tim
Sweeney, Phil Varner

Fall 2001
Design Development and
Construction Detailing

*School of Architecture
Students (ARCH 531 PV
House Detailing
and Construction):*

Charlotte Barrows,
Alexander Butler, Dickson
Fogleman, Joshua
Galloway, Brian Gerich,
Kirk Jansen, Chris Kroner,
Yang Liu, Danny MacNelly,
Stephen Nielson, Kathleen
Robertson, Adam Ruffin,
Ben Spencer, Ben
Thompson, Jennifer
Trompetter, Greg Vogler,
Mary Moore Wallinger,
Justin Weisser

*School of Engineering
and Applied Science
Students (ENGR 495
PV House Detailing
and Construction):*

George Allman, Tyson
Baldridge, Jason
Campbell, Dave Click,
Sara Corbett, Ben Dorrier,
Derek Drish, John Eterno,
Kelly Fish, Shannon
Graeber, Lucas Hoffmann,
Mary Katherine Mawyer,
Keith Miller, Martin Miller,
Tom Nelson, Dan
Podhajny, Tim Sweeney,
Tsedenia Woldehanna

Spring 2002
Construction Documents
and Construction

*School of Architecture
Students (ARCH 402
Architectural Design–
Sun Studio2):*

Meredith Atthowe,
Dawn Balsam, Charlotte
Barrows, Rachel Baxter,
Josh Dannenberg, Emily
Mallinak, Scott McGihon,
Teddy Nelson, Emily Rhee,
Lisa Rauhecker, Andrew
Scheidt, Jean Suh

School of Architecture Students (ARCH 782, ARCH 870 and LAR 811 Independent Study):

Ross Altheimer, Jeffrey Aten, Andy Burdick, Alexander Butler, Colin Davis, Kent Dougherty, Dickson Fogleman, Joshua Galloway, Brian Gerich, Anne James, Kirk Jansen, Danny MacNelly, Stephen Nielson, Kathleen Robertson, Adam Ruffin, Ben Spencer, Greg Vogler, Justin Weisser, Derek Windels

School of Architecture Students (ARCH 582 Architectural Crafts):

Meredith Atthowe, Tolga Baydar, Sam Beadel, Irene Boland, Jennifer Currier, Breck Gastinger, Kirk Jansen, Hana Kim, Emily Mottolese, Stephen Nielson, Derek Windels

Graduate School of Arts and Sciences, Drama Department Students (ARCH 582 Architectural Crafts):

Susannah Barnes, Jenny Sawyers

School of Engineering and Applied Science Students (ENGR 499 Special Topics):

Tyson Baldridge, David Britz, Dave Click, Sara Corbett, Ben Dorrier, Derek Drish, John Eterno, Kelly Fish, Shannon Graeber, Jessica Hess, Charles Kasenge, Matthew Keller, Mee Jee Lee, Mary Katherine Mawyer, Martin Miller, Tom Nelson, Dan Podhajny, Tim Sweeney, Phil Varner, Tsedenia Woldehanna, Andy Wong

College of Arts and Sciences, Economics Department Students (accounting):

Bill Click, Ryan Han

Summer and Early Fall 2002 Construction

School of Architecture Students:

Stephen Allen, Jeffrey Aten, Dawn Balsam, Charlotte Barrows, Rachel Baxter, Sam Beadel, Alexander Butler, Josh Dannenberg, Soren DeNiord, Theo Diamond, Emily Farnham, Dickson Fogleman, Joshua Galloway, Brian Gerich,

Susan Hughes, Kirk Jansen, Ursula Larson, Danny MacNelly, Scott McGihon, Emily Mottolese, Noel Murphy, Teddy Nelson, Bryce Powell, Adam Ruffin, Georgianna Salz, Andrew Scheidt, Will Sparks, Ben Spencer, Jennifer Trompetter, Justin Weisser

School of Engineering and Applied Science Students:

Tyson Baldridge, Paul Biu, Dave Click, Ben Dorrier, John Eterno, Matt Green, Richard Hansen, Martin Miller, Tom Nelson, Dan Podhajny, Tim Sweeney, Leigh Thelen

College of Arts and Sciences:

Mitch Anstey, Jason Carey

Community Volunteers:

David Booth, Evan Childress, Ed Click, Ben Clough, Bo Daniels, Ed Ford, Catherine Greiner, Peter Jackson, Brendan James, Bill Jobes, Amy Keling, Yolande Landry, Brooks Marshall, Catie Marshall, Susan Marshall, Annie Quast, David Rasmussen, Brandy Savarese, Gabe Silver, Jessie Silver, Shawn Srubbe, Tom Von Hemert, Karen Van Lengen, Sara Vieweg, Jim Welty,

Heather West, James Wilson, Stephen Wilson

Spring 2003 through Spring 2005 Monitoring

School of Engineering and Applied Science Students:

Jacqueline Ainsztein, Karen Buenconsejo, Shana Craft, Fabienne Gaillard, Richard Hansen, Matthew Kindig, Jennifer Laney, Susan Larson, Ashley Lewit, Justin Nelson, Daniel Mask, Ana Ramcharan, Landon Shoop, Ondrej Sklenar, Leigh Thelen, Justin Williamson

Community and Additional University Advisors:

Jeff Yago, J.R. Yago & Associates, Consulting Engineers, photovoltaic expert

Bill Jobes, builder, renewable energy expert

Ben Clough and David Rasmussen, builders

Tom Kavounas and Jeff Saul, Albemarle Heating and Air

Theo van Groll, Former Associate Dean for Student Affairs, School of Architecture

David Williams, Wood Shop Manager, School of Architecture

Kirk Martini, Associate Professor, School of Architecture

Jason Johnson, Visiting Assistant Professor, School of Architecture

Jack Horn Sr., Jack Horn Jr., Joe Milby, Ted Horn, Martin-Horn General Contractors

Mark Schuyler, principal, Mark Schuyler Lighting Design

Eric Thompson, Earthstar Energy Systems

Denwood Milby, DMWPV Consulting Structural Engineers

Keith Rittenhouse, DMWPV Consulting Structural Engineers

Sara Osborne, landscape architect; partner, Q&O Design

Mitch King, Old Mill Power Company

Robert Crowell, 2RW Consulting Engineers

Rosanne Simeone, Lecturer, School of Engineering and Applied Science

Additional Thanks To:

School of Architecture:

Karen Van Lengen,
Dean and Edward E.
Elson Professor

Judith Kinnard,
Associate Professor and
Former Chair, Architecture

Bill Sherman,
Associate Professor and
Chair, Architecture and
Landscape Architecture

Charles Menefee,
Associate Professor and
Director of Architecture

Edward Ford,
Associate Professor

W.G. Clark,
Professor, Architecture

Robin Dripps,
Professor, Architecture

Peter Waldman,
Professor, Architecture

Nataly Gattegno,
Visiting Assistant
Professor, Architecture

Cecilia Hernandez,
Lecturer, Architecture;
partner, Formwork Design

Nicholas de Monchaux,
Assistant Professor,
Architecture

Earl Mark,
Associate Professor
and Director of
Computer Technologies

Elizabeth Meyer,
Associate Professor and
Former Chair,
Landscape Architecture

Julie Bargmann,
Associate Professor,
Director of
Landscape Architecture

Nancy Takahashi,
Lecturer, Landscape
Architecture

Timothy Beatley,
Associate Professor,
Urban and
Environmental Planning

Elizabeth Fortune,
Associate Dean
for Administration
and Finance

Susan Ketron,
School of Architecture
Foundation Director

Jayne Riew,
Former Associate Director
of Development and
Alumni Relations

Michele Monger,
Development and
Alumni Relations

Jennifer Hitchcock,
Department of
Architecture and
Landscape Architecture

Jake Thackston,
Manager of
Computer Technologies

John Vigour,
Computer Technologies

Eric Field,
Computer Technologies

Michelle Allen,
Business Office

Lisa Benton,
Business Office

**School of Engineering and
Applied Science:**

Richard Miksad,
Former Dean and Thomas
M. Linville Professor

Taylor Beard,
Associate Professor,
Mechanical and
Aerospace Engineering

Harry Powell,
Engineer

Mircea Stan,
Associate Professor,
Electrical and
Computer Engineering

Mary Smith,
Assistant Dean for
Finance and Budget

Tom Connors,
Vice President, Virginia
Engineering Foundation

George Cahen,
Virginia Engineering
Foundation

Josie Pipkin, Virginia
Engineering Foundation

Amy Siddons, Virginia
Engineering Foundation

Mary Lane,
Undergraduate Programs

Priscilla Mezick,
Undergraduate Programs

Nellie Koon,
Budget Office

Phyllis Bibb,
Budget Office

Mary Smith,
Budget Office

Elsewhere:

Karen Marshall

Maite Brandt-Pearce

Robert Nichols,
partner, Formwork Design

Dave Watkins,
Engineer

Tom VonHemert

Barry Schnoor

Stu Armstrong,
Piedmont Housing
Alliance

Mark Watson,
Piedmont Housing
Alliance

Peter Loach,
Piedmont Housing
Alliance

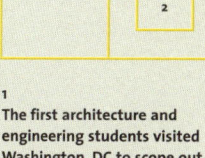

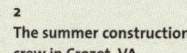

1
The first architecture and
engineering students visited
Washington, DC to scope out
the site of the competition

2
The summer construction
crew in Crozet, VA

Results

- Second Place Overall
- First Place in Design and Livability Contest
- First Place in the Energy Balance Conte
- Special Citation from the American Institute of Architects
- BP Solar "Progressive Award" for the most forward-thinking team
- Honor Award in the student category of 2003 Entablature Website Design Awards

Information on the contests of the 2002 Solar Decathlon
can be found at www.solardecathlon.org.

Contest 1: Design and Livability

1
University of Delaware

2
University of Texas at Austin

3
University of Maryland

4
**University of Missouri at Rolla
and Rolla Technical Institute**

Team	Points	Ranking
University of Virginia	200.000	1
University of Puerto Rico	184.615	2
University of Texas at Austin	169.231	3
Virginia Tech	153.846	4
University of Colorado at Boulder	134.462	5
Auburn University	105.692	6
Tuskegee University	88.308	7
Carnegie Mellon University	75.077	8
University of Maryland	74.923	9
University of Missouri - Rolla / Rolla Technical Institute	61.538	10
Crowder College	46.154	11
University of Delaware	30.769	12
Texas A&M	0.000	13
University of North Carolina - Charlotte	-48.615	14

Contest 2: Design Presentation and Simulation

Team	Points	Ranking
Virginia Tech	83.658	1
Carnegie Mellon University	82.886	2
University of Maryland	73.651	3
University of Puerto Rico	72.086	4
University of Colorado at Boulder	65.905	5
University of Texas at Austin	64.907	6
University of Virginia	63.662	7
Auburn University	61.240	8
University of Delaware	52.861	9
University of North Carolina - Charlotte	40.093	10
Crowder College	38.078	11
Tuskegee University	32.168	12
Texas A&M	30.443	13
University of Missouri - Rolla / Rolla Technical Institute	7.750	14

Contest 3: Graphics and Communication

Team	Points	Ranking
University of Colorado at Boulder	93.077	1
Auburn University	80.769	2
University of Texas at Austin	70.769	3
Virginia Tech	60.769	4
University of Virginia	60.769	4
Crowder College	59.231	5
University of Maryland	58.462	6
University of Puerto Rico	52.308	7
Tuskegee University	43.846	8
University of Delaware	34.615	9
University of Missouri - Rolla / Rolla Technical Institute	29.231	10
Texas A&M	27.692	11
Carnegie Mellon University	23.846	12
University of North Carolina - Charlotte	4.615	13

Contest 4: The Comfort Zone

Team	Points	Ranking
University of Colorado at Boulder	84.423	1
University of Maryland	68.462	2
Auburn University	68.462	3
University of Delaware	65.577	4
Crowder College	64.615	5
University of Missouri - Rolla / Rolla Technical Institute	60.385	6
Virginia Tech	54.808	7
Tuskegee University	53.846	8
University of Virginia	50.577	9
University of Texas at Austin	48.654	10
Carnegie Mellon University	35.769	11
University of North Carolina - Charlotte	31.346	12
University of Puerto Rico	28.077	13
Texas A&M	0.000	14

Contest 5: Refrigeration

Team	Points	Ranking
University of Missouri - Rolla / Rolla Technical Institute	90.769	1
Crowder College	82.692	2
Auburn University	77.308	3
University of Virginia	76.538	4
University of Maryland	68.077	5
University of Colorado at Boulder	59.615	6
University of North Carolina - Charlotte	55.769	7
University of Puerto Rico	50.385	8
University of Delaware	50.385	9
Virginia Tech	47.692	10
University of Texas at Austin	47.308	11
Tuskegee University	45.000	12
Carnegie Mellon University	31.538	13
Texas A&M	0.000	14

Contest 6: Hot Water

Team	Points	Ranking
University of Maryland	95.000	1
Auburn University	88.462	2
University of Missouri - Rolla / Rolla Technical Institute	83.077	3
Virginia Tech	80.385	4
University of Colorado at Boulder	77.692	5
University of Puerto Rico	77.015	6
Crowder College	75.769	7
University of Delaware	73.846	8
University of Virginia	72.308	9
University of Texas at Austin	71.923	10
Carnegie Mellon University	61.538	11
Tuskegee University	45.000	12
University of North Carolina - Charlotte	40.000	13
Texas A&M	35.000	14

Contest 7: Energy Balance

Team	Points	Ranking
Auburn University	100.000	1
University of Colorado at Boulder	100.000	1
Crowder College	100.000	1
University of Maryland	100.000	1
University of Virginia	100.000	1
University of Missouri - Rolla / Rolla Technical Institute	88.889	2
University of Delaware	77.778	3
University of Texas at Austin	66.667	4
University of Puerto Rico	55.556	5
University of North Carolina - Charlotte	44.444	6
Virginia Tech	33.333	7
Tuskegee University	22.222	8
Carnegie Mellon University	11.111	9
Texas A&M	00.000	10

Contest 8: Lighting

Team	Points	Ranking
Crowder College	96.923	1
Virginia Tech	92.000	2
University of Colorado at Boulder	90.128	3
University of Virginia	88.385	4
University of Maryland	87.679	5
University of Puerto Rico	85.731	6
Auburn University	85.321	7
University of Texas at Austin	76.026	8
University of Delaware	71.974	9
University of Missouri - Rolla / Rolla Technical Institute	69.577	10
Carnegie Mellon University	69.103	11
Tuskegee University	64.782	12
University of North Carolina - Charlotte	56.372	13
Texas A&M	23.000	14

1
University of Puerto Rico

2
Crowder College

3
Virginia Polytechnic and State University

4
The UVA team crosses the "finish line" at the end of the getting around contest

5
University of Colorado at Boulder

66

Contest 9: Home Business

Team	Points	Ranking
Virginia Tech	100.00	1
Auburn University	92.308	2
University of Colorado at Boulder	84.615	3
University of Missouri - Rolla / Rolla Technical Institute	76.923	4
University of Maryland	69.231	5
Crowder College	61.538	6
University of Virginia	53.846	7
University of Puerto Rico	46.154	8
Carnegie Mellon University	38.462	9
Tuskegee University	30.769	10
University of Texas at Austin	23.077	11
University of Delaware	15.385	12
University of North Carolina - Charlotte	7.692	13
Texas A&M	0.000	14

Contest 10: Getting Around

Team	Points	Ranking
Virginia Tech	100.00	1
Auburn University	92.308	2
University of Colorado at Boulder	84.615	3
University of Missouri - Rolla / Rolla Technical Institute	76.923	4
University of Maryland	69.231	5
Crowder College	61.538	6
University of Virginia	53.846	7
University of Puerto Rico	46.154	8
Carnegie Mellon University	38.462	9
Tuskegee University	30.769	10
University of Texas at Austin	23.077	11
University of Delaware	15.385	12
University of North Carolina - Charlotte	7.692	13
Texas A&M	0.000	14

Overall

Team	Points	Ranking
University of Colorado at Boulder	875.302	1
University of Virginia	848.521	2
Auburn University	840.330	3
University of Maryland	777.921	4
Virginia Tech	777.901	5
Crowder College	725.001	6
University of Puerto Rico	712.216	7
University of Texas at Austin	709.330	8
University of Missouri - Rolla / Rolla Technical Institute	652.241	9
University of Delaware	543.446	10
Tuskegee University	513.377	11
Carnegie Mellon University	502.023	12
University of North Carolina - Charlotte	251.958	13
Texas A&M	122.802	14

Media Quotes

"Amassing the largest score for design and livability, the University of Virginia team built a house with an exterior of reclaimed copper cladding and [louvers] made from shipping crates. The interiors are made with maple paneling and have floor-to-ceiling windows and [glass] tile. The walls move to let in sun and heat in winter and to create breezes and shade in summer. The mirror dish on the roof feeds daylight through fiber-optic glass tubes for diffusion into the rooms. A gutter system catches rainwater and feeds it to potted plants."

The New York Times, Amanda Griscom Little, October 3rd, 2002

"The University of Virginia team hand-crafted its long box as if it were a jewel, reshaping recycled materials as ordinary as wooden shipping pallets and as unusual as [bluestone] panels discarded from the terraces of Thomas Jefferson's Rotunda."

Washington Post, Benjamin Forgery, architecture critic, September 28th, 2002

"The UVA house, clad in reclaimed copper beneath slatted rain screens made from salvaged wood from shipping pallets, and topped by a small rooftop garden, balances a warm, organic look with a modernist pedigree."

Washington Post, Weekend section, Caroline Kettlewell, September 27th, 2002

"But the team from the University of Virginia is proud of its silence [referring to the lack of a gas powered generator during the late stages of construction]. As student Adam Ruffin told us, the team is already working exclusively with solar power. Voice of Adam Ruffin: 'We are showing that you can not only live in a solar house, but that you can build one.'"

National Public Radio, Weekend Edition, Scott Simon, September 28th, 2002

"The University of Virginia group won the design and livability category— which measured innovation and aesthetics— with sensuous copper and wood cladding, rooftop photovoltaics, and an elegant design. In devising a climate-responsive house, the team seized on the idea of a hard exterior unfolding to reveal a highly refined, nicely detailed interior."

Metropolis Magazine, Kira L. Gould, January 2003

"The University of Virginia entry [was] an intriguing modernist structure the size of a large mobile home framed in engineered lumber and clad in reclaimed copper roofing."

Architecture Magazine, Bradford McKee, November 2002

"The University of Virginia won the design contest by a unanimous vote. In a later phone interview, [Architecture juror Glenn] Murcutt commented that, 'Virginia had a design that showed that a solar home is not just about plunking a panel on top. It must be as poetic as it is rational. It must consider every aspect of sustainability, from the building materials to the insulation and ductwork to the way light is used. It must be whole-building sustainable design, and all those components must integrated in an elegant way.'"

"Green architects believe that all solar structures must be approached holistically: Before a designer even considers putting solar panels on the roof, she has to create the most efficient structure possible. What, after all, would be the point of buying expensive PV panels to power an air conditioner or heat a house if the fruit of all those hard-won electrons leaks out of poorly insulated walls and windows? And why put loads of light fixtures in the house (and expend energy to power them) if you can design the home to have abundant natural lighting?"

"The Virginia team covered all its bases in terms of super-insulated walls and windows and energy-efficient appliances, and then they took the idea of sustainability one step further. They used reclaimed copper cladding and wooden trellises made from shipping crates for the exteriors. On the interiors they maximized natural lighting by installing floor-to-ceiling insulated glass on the entire south-facing wall and adding movable walls to create shade in the summer and let in light and warmth in the winter. They used maple paneling and translucent [glass] tiles on the walls to create a constant cozy glow. To add some high-tech splash, they put a mirror dish on the roof that collects daylight and feeds it through fiber-optic tubes to the interior for non-electric lighting. There was even a 'smart wall'—a large computer monitor in the front hall that controls all the appliances in the house. The team programmed it to change colors according to the temperature of the house (it blushes pink when the houses is warm and turns blue when the house is cool) to give a sensory understanding of how the house works."

"'The future is right here on the mall right now, all these schools and all these students,' said John Quale, professor of architecture at the University of Virginia, 'I firmly believe that more significant change will happen in the future of architecture with this generation of students than any other. These students really believe that ethical issues and aesthetic issues can't be separated from each other.'"

"The way the topics are being taught is different, too. Solar design is merging the disciplines of architecture and engineering. In the past, architects have always hired engineers as consultants, but a whole-building green design requires collaboration and a multidisciplinary approach from the outset."

Grist Magazine, Amanda Griscom Little, October 30th, 2002, www.grist.org

Sponsors

Major Sponsor

University of Virginia

Martin-Horn
General Contractors

Elwood R. Quesada
Educational Foundation

UVA Alumni Association,
Class of 1995

Anonymous

Sponsor

Albemarle Heating
& Air Inc.

ASE Americas

Charlottesville Glass
and Mirror

Comfort Line Windows
& Doors

Commonwealth of
Virginia, Department
of Mines, Minerals
and Energy

Dunimis Technology Inc.
(J.R. Yago & Associates)

Fair Play Foundation

Rexel Branch
Electrical Supplies

W.A. Lynch Roofing

Weyerhaeuser Building
Materials and Trus Joist

Weyerhaeuser Company
Foundation

Supporter

Advantech Automation

Allied Concrete

American Hydrotech

Asko

Belfer Lighting

Better Living

Blue Ridge
Radiant Systems

Carolina Staylite

Cavalier Computers

Rose and Robert
Capon Fund

The Ceiling &
Floor Shop, Inc.

Comfort Foam Insulation

Compass Contracting

Concorde Batteries

Coran Capshaw

Creative Conservation

Cross Automation

Crutchfield Corporation

Dell Computer
Corporation

DMWPV Consulting
Structural Engineers

DuPont Tyvek

DuPont Foundation

Earthstar Energy Systems

Emory Knoll Farms

Endurawood

Enhancement Electronics

Gaston & Wyatt

Mr. and Mrs. William H.
Goodwin, Jr.

Home Depot

John D. Howell &
Associates

Hybrid Lighting
Partnership

Integris Metals

Landstar Heavy Haul

Lutron Electronics

Marguerite D. MacNelly

Marriott Corporation –
Key Bridge Marriott

National Instruments

N.B. Handy Company

Noland Plumbing Supply

Northland Forest Products

Oak Ridge National
Laboratory

Old Mill Power Company

Philips Lighting

Rehau North America

Resun Leasing

Ronstan International Inc.

Simpson Strong Tie

Sun Frost

3M

Tom's of Maine

Triangle Tube Tanks

TruStile Doors

Two Seas Metalworks

2RW Consulting Engineers

UVA School of Architecture Design Council

UVA Student Council

Velux Skylights

Virginia House Movers

William McDonough and Partners

ALC Copies

Bailey Printing, Inc.

Jessica Barrows and Andrew Beebe

The Benevolent Society of the Goat

Blue Ridge Graphics

Creative Automation

Dankoff Solar Products, Inc.

Dr. Steve and Sandi Dannenberg

Dickies–The Williamson-Dickie Mfg. Co.

Encore Decor, Washington DC

Trina English

Envirospec

Fisher & Paykel Appliances

Florida Heat Pump

Foods of All Nations

Hafele America

Home Media

Hy-Tech Thermal Solutions

Integral Yoga and Natural Foods

J. Michael Jarvis

Lowe's Home Improvement Warehouse — Charlottesville store

Cathy Mares Custom Sewing

Ron Martin Appliances

Mechanical Equipment Sales

Monarch Metal Fabrication, Inc.

Naturalemporium.com

Quality Welding

David Rose Company

Safe Building Solutions

Sears

Jay R. Smith Mfg. Co.

Richard and Alice Spencer

Subway – Crozet, Virginia branch

Tridonic, Inc

UVA School of Architecture, Office of Development and Alumni Affairs

UVA School of Engineering and Applied Science, Virginia Engineering Foundation

UVA University Development Office

UVA School of Architecture, AIAS

Roger Voisinet, Re/Max Realty Specialists

Esmeralda J. Ward

Whole Foods

About the Author

John D. Quale is Assistant Professor of Architecture at the University of Virginia School of Architecture where he has taught architectural design studios, building technology courses and photography for the past five years. Quale served as the architecture advisor and coordinator for the 2002 UVa Solar Decathlon Team, and is currently the project director for ecoMOD, an interdisciplinary design/build project focused on ecologically based modular housing for low income families.

Photo Credits